SCATTERED CHAPTERS

Scattered Chapters

new & selected poems **Baron Wormser**

Sarabande  Books

LOUISVILLE, KENTUCKY

Library of Congress Cataloging-in-Publication Data

Wormser, Baron.
Scattered chapters : new and selected poems / Baron Wormser. — 1st ed.
    p.   cm.
ISBN-13: 978-1-932511-61-1 (pbk. : acid-free paper)
I. Title.
PS3573.O693S28 2008
811'.54—dc21   2007025985

Cover art: *Lyric Suite #23*, 1965, by Robert Motherwell. © Dedalus Foundation, Inc./Licensed by VAGA, New York, NY

Cover and text design by Charles Casey Martin

Manufactured in Canada
This book is printed on acid-free paper.

Sarabande Books is a nonprofit literary organization.

THE KENTUCKY ARTS COUNCIL

The Kentucky Arts Council, a state agency in the Commerce Cabinet, provides operational support funding for Sarabande Books with state tax dollars and federal funding from the National Endowment for the Arts, which believes that a great nation deserves great art.

For Janet

. . . through it all

Contents

From *The White Words* (1983)

From *Good Trembling* (1985)

From *Atoms, Soul Music and Other Poems* (1989)

From *When* (1997)

From *Mulroney and Others* (2000)

From *Subject Matter* (2004)

From *Carthage* (2005)

A Note from the Author

Here and there, I have taken the opportunity to revise various previously published poems. Special thanks to James Provencher, Howard Levy, Jay Franzel and Richard Miles for their input.

Grateful acknowledgment is made to the editors and publishers of the following journals in which new poems first appeared: *Sewanee Review, Chautauqua Literary Journal, Off the Coast, Manhattan Review, Bryant Literary Review, Nightsun, Rivendell, Paris Review, Tar River Poetry, Connecticut Review, Two Rivers Review, Barrow Street, Prairie Schooner, Amoskeag, Columbia Poetry Review, Green Mountains Review, Mipoesias.*

"On the Lawn of the Kinsman" first appeared in *The Breath of Parted Lips: Voices from the Robert Frost Place, Volume II.* "Cheerful" and "The Pump" appeared in *Contemporary Poetry of New England.*

SCATTERED CHAPTERS

New Poems

Falling

Snow buries cars and yews and garbage cans
Beside the dirty beige garage and sits so
Delicately on the unwavering maple limbs.
A girl of ten who cannot sleep for
The excitement and enchantment of it
Watches the great specks falling through the globe
Of yellow light that is the streetlight nearest
To her house, the house in which she lies in bed
Protected from the dreamy descent of the endless sky,
Protected from the wet and cold. Safe.

She feels her heart beating and it seems loud,
Louder than it should be but then she thinks how
It's something she never truly listens to, she's never
That still or the world around her isn't that still.
It's scary, this heart inside her chest that lives
Its own life, that one day will stop and she,
As they say in the tales she reads, will be no more.

Come morning, it may still be snowing.
A friendly important man on the radio
Will announce there is no school today.
She will be free to sculpt the drifts
And prairies into igloos, tunnels and walls,
To place snow on her tongue and taste
The cool airiness, to feel the sting
Of wind-sifted flakes on her face.

Now, though, she goes to the window
And stares and stares. The snow feels like the heart
Of the whole world, falling, falling and perfect.

Calendar (1956)

Rabinowitz tries to crawl
Inside the numbers.
He multiplies, for instance,
The days of the year times
A fortunate life span
And arrives at an impressive
Figure—Twenty-five thousand
And five hundred.
Still, it is a poor unprepossessing
Number beside the tree
From which millions of leaves fell.

Rabinowitz sits with a calendar
Which he fills in
With names such as Shulamith
Or Schmuel or Hersh or Reva.
Each day of the calendar
Gets a name and he says
The name when he looks
At the calendar in the morning,
A sound he makes
For the sake of sound,
A wafer of prayer,
A blue speck of feeling.

During the last week of December
He fills in every day
Of the next year with names.

He dreams of thin black hair,
Frizzy brown hair, half-smiles,
Grimaces, sobs, small fingers,
Fat fingers, thumbs,
Old people and children,
Loud voices, murmurs.

This is the calendar
That awaits a new religion,
Braver than the previous ones.
Today is Tsaureh-The-Baker's-Wife Day.
The Jews have their years.
The Gentiles have theirs.
Eternity cares nothing.

Existence plods on like
A trek to nowhere
But Rabinowitz has spoken for each day.
He dreams of reddish curly hair,
Dimples, long necks,
Dear serious soulful eyes
That bury oblivion.

Labor

I spent a couple of years during my undestined
Twenties on a north woods acreage
That grew, as the locals poetically phrased it,
"Stones and rocks." I loved it.

No real insulation in the old farmhouse,
Which meant ten cords of hardwood,
Which meant a muscled mantra of cutting,
Yarding, splitting, stacking and burning.

I was the maul coming down *kerchunk*
On the round of maple; I was the hellacious
Screeching saw; I was the fire.
I was fiber and grew imperceptibly.

I lost interest in everything except for trees.
Career, ambition and politics bored me.
I loved putting on my steel-toe, lace-up
Work boots in the morning. I loved the feel

Of my feet on grass slick with dew or frost
Or ice-skimmed mud or crisp snow crust.
I loved the moment after I felled a tree
When it was still again and I felt the awe

Of what I had done and awe for the tree that had
Stretched toward the sky for silent decades.

On Saturday night the regulars who had worked
In the woods forever mocked me as I limped into

The bar out on the state highway. "Workin' hard
There, sonny, or more like hardly workin'?"
I cradled my bottle between stiff raw hands,
Felt a pinching tension in the small of my back,

Inhaled ripe sweat, damp flannel,
Cheap whiskey then nodded—a happy fool.
They grinned back. Through their proper
Scorn I could feel it. They loved it too.

for Hayden Carruth

The O's

My grandfather is lying in the hospital bed
Listening to the radio every night.
It's the second week of the season; he's an Orioles fan
Ever since the O's came to Baltimore
In 1954—but it's 1988 and they lose game
After game after game after game after game.

My grandfather's face looks like a hardball hit it—
Black and blue and yellow. It's cancer
That tie dyes you in muted shades so you
Wind up looking like a hung-over toad,
Which is no big thing to my grandfather
Who drank too much and smoked way too much—

Cigars—but never was vain, never was
A look-in-the-mirror type but always grabbed
His hat and said he was ready. Grandpa's got a month
At the most, according to the oncologist who spoke as if
He were putting down a deuce at Pimlico.
Grandpa knows this, which is to say it's not

The dogwoods or forsythia or magnolias he's going to miss,
Not the newly mown grass or the crab soup his long time
Paramour, Bessie, still makes even though Grandpa can't
Eat much of anything anymore; he's a slave to tubes.
It's the losing streak that he can't abide because they're
Bound to win one, sooner or later the announcer's

Voice is going to take off into the ozone of announcer
Excitement with a whoosh and a wallop
And the curse will be over. Losing is for losers and Grandpa,
Who has spent his life making and taking bets,
Hates losers. Inning by inning we sit listening
And Grandpa knows it's stupid, he knows

He's dying and he should be thinking about last things
But he doesn't know anything about last things.
He hasn't been in a shul in fifty years and his
Only religion is the worship of the female body.
He's an idolater. A sack of calcified lust. I turn off
The radio and the nurse looks in on the mostly gone man
And his grandson sitting in the wan, fluorescent light
That could have come from *Macbeth* it's so
Grievous and spectral and unhealthy. Death light.
We aren't saying anything, but Grandpa's still alive
And though the O's have lost another there's still
Tomorrow. Grandpa closes his eyes when the nurse

Comes in with a little paper cup filled with pills
And I say that I've got to head home and grade some themes.
His watery hesitant eyes open because he knows
He might not see me again; he might not hear another
"Here's the first pitch." "We're not finished yet," he rasps
And I smile a smile I can't help because he's right.

Cheerful

Not passable, not special, not ostensible,
But cheerful, as in rising in the winter darkness
Of a northern morning and, while walking down
The worn bare-wood stairs to the kitchen and
  The cold cook stove, whistling

For the sake of being in a relatively warm body,
For the sake of sliding fingers along the smooth rail,
For the sake of being eager to start a fire exactly
As she liked to start it with shredded
  Newspaper, split kindling

And a bit of birch bark and there it went—
The glow, a tiny whiff of smoke and the ardent
Promise of heat. Cheerful in her mind that knew
Which pan to take down, how much butter to put
  In that pan, how many days'

Butter was left in the fridge, how much butter
Cost at the A&P, cheerful for looking out the window
At ice-whiskered nothingness and knowing there would be
A day, an event sponsored by galaxies, God
  Or gravity—choose one or choose

Them all. Sunlight was a hymn, though she knew better
Than to tell the local preacher. Half-overalled
Husband cranky, the boys cuffing one other and muttering

Mockeries beneath their sleep-furred breath
　　And she cheerful to their faces

Like an opera singer exiled by catastrophe
To some cow town who rose in the shivery blank morning
And sat on the edge of her gray narrow bed
And began—despite herself and because of herself—
　　To whistle an intractable aria.

Kinderscene

I lie in a cave
Beneath the massive mahogany dining room table

To my self I sing a song
Of syllables that rattle like beans

Okie flokie shu ma nah
Okie flokie shu ma nah
My voice keens warbles wavers

Upstairs my mother is reading in a book
My father works late in a large building

I examine the table's underside
Much rougher than its glossy top

I raise my hands as if to hold it up
It is a roof and I a village
I am bells and cows and wind in rustling grass

Then I am a child
Lying in the silent dark
A distant syllable in a distant song

Homage to Robert Frank (Three Photographs)

One: Procession, Barcelona, 1952

Our breath is sour and we shuffle like cows.
Our horns bleat like farts after dinner.
One two, one two, one two. We march for death,
For how beautiful death was, for the deaths

We dealt, for the dictator who salutes us.
Memory can make a man pensive but our caps
And tunics maintain a finical dignity.
Because we have done with the whining

Of the living, we seize the bronze clarion
Of anniversaries. We have done with the vanquished,
With the pathos women exchange and the ragged
Cries of children. We march for death, for the one
Who understands us and our wretched music
That makes no one happy and never stops.

Two: Caerau, Wales

Rackety children whoop in the gray cold
For any joy the sky might send them.
Their faces proclaim the pleasure of
Careening feeling—moments are toys.

They smile crookedly for these unspent hours
And the worn, chthonic hills
That give no comfort and share no promise.
They smile against the inevitable,

The dullest Monday imaginable,
When you are kept inside so the surly
Clock can scold, "Beware," when curtains
Efface windows and stairs go nowhere.
This day, however, displays no regret.
Someday it will but not now, not yet.

Three: Barcelona—Cigarette Vendor

Dignity is a thick feather bed.
When death comes to call, he is polite.
"How are you, *señora?* Too bad, too bad."
He clicks his long tongue sadly.

Happiness scampers down the dusty street—
A stupid puppy planting paws
On a blouse's gentle white glow.
She clutches her woven basket; her eyes

Window the bleary ebb of her soul.
The stubborn coins wish to congregate,
A thin weight that bears her indifferent heart
Into evening's depths when she lies down
On rushes, straw mat or earth and listens
For the dirge that was heard at her birth.

Locks

I click off the lamps,
Damp the wood stove,
Check the locks

As if the house were a fortress.
Husband and wife, all day
We have been unto ourselves

With one another—
Oblique love quilted with habit.
I search for a missing scissors;

You know where it dwells.
Why is the Protestant ethic
So intractable, you marvel.

Looking up from a plate of greens,
I semi-explicate.
No one's come in today

Out of the cold or the heat
From a car or a star.
We've kept the same faces

While spading up grace,
Sowing calm kisses
Where they might prosper.

The locks are stoic.
The lights are out.
We lie in bed and touch.

Our voices murmur.
Devotion is the strangest longing,
The one that is satisfied.

Class of '65 (1990)

"The lights are going out already," my mother sighs
In reference to some of my classmates from
　　Sturtevant High School who
Though they would have been only in their forties
　　Are gone:

The casualties of AIDS, heart attacks, car crashes
And the common cancers that play the pining ghosts
　　In the polymer paradise.
I nod in agreement although I'm in another room
　　Eating

Slices of American cheese and pimiento loaf
While perusing an article about a movie star
　　Who drowned in his Saturnalia-
Sized swimming pool. I reflect that you don't see
　　Mortality's

Face much in the glossies where life looks like one
Long, languorous orgasm of cleavage, jeans and vodka.
　　Nor do you see the Dance of Death
Strutting its leering stuff in the malls and outlet stores,
　　Banging

Bones on hubcaps and metal trashcan covers
And keening the contralto funk of time.
　　My mother, meanwhile, goes back

To the crossword puzzle in the *TV Guide* and then
   To the tube

Where even when people are trying to be rational
They're yelling. They're always some decibels
   Above polite conversation, to say
Nothing of the whispers that are the soft
   Coins

Of our distressed humanity. My mother leaves me thinking
About Chuck Meola and Binky Smith and Iris Prendergast.
   For immeasurable seconds
Their pure adolescent incandescence vibrates
   Like one

Of those back-of-the-classroom raspberries startling
The reverie of a dusty afternoon. In the other room,
   The TV chortles and brays.
My vision vanishes; the lights go out amid relentless
   Laughter.

Remission

The radiology tech measures death's
Progress, wheels a machine in place
Like a siege gun from World War One.

Calibrations give commands but
Shells fall on the wrong soldiers.
Voiceless, they gaze at blindness.

She sits up in her cold strict bed as if
The good explosions could be heard.
Target and map, she silently traces
Fingers over soft peaceful skin.

She thrills to her perpetual birthday, eager
To caress the slightest anniversary.

Contempt is the pride of poignancy.

She catches herself looking ahead.

She envisions the poor soldiers who halt
For a pale second before they clamber
Over trench tops. Bullets trace a lazy swathe.

Oratory is hopeful mumbling.

The day's treatment done, she walks out
A door that is alive on both sides.

She sings her love for her body.
It is a selfish song and terribly wise.

for Sherry

Released

When the parent club let go of Bobby Dodson
With a month left in that minor league's
Bad-buses-and-thunderstorms season,
He made the ritual call home,
Hollering "I'm done" into the receiver, hanging up
Before his mother could begin dispensing comfort,
Before his girlfriend hauled out his scrapbooks,
Before his father grabbed a stale panatela.

In the clubhouse everyone mouthed the *good luck* things
You say to someone who's hit the wall at Double A.
Every player knew the scenarios:
Which base to throw to,
When to take a longer lead off first,
What pitch likely was coming next.
The trouble was the psyche inside the uniform,
That was helpless as a barely feathered chick,
That was thinking positively in the middle
Of the worst slump, that could only try harder,
That kept telling jokes when guys' arms went dead
Or they pulled a hamstring or broke a bone. True believers,
Good old boys, overachievers, diamonds that stayed rough—
    take your pick.

He couldn't hit a slider. Words were bullshit.

The parking lot pocked with red and blue, second-engine
Mustangs and Trans-Ams. Dudemobiles.

His own car smelled like a tannery, a cheeseburger and
A bedroom with no windows, but, as he threw his gear
In the backseat, he found himself looking forward to
The driving—the standard shifts, the automatic turns.

John Winthrop

The prior evening there had been a wind upon
The water that was devilish, a punishing tempest...

And when a man appeared before John Winthrop,
God's vicegerent, to say that it was the body
Of Winthrop's son that had washed up nearby,
Winthrop looked at the man as if to read his face.

"Each death," he noted, "speaks to our extremity."

He had been sitting and writing a letter back to England
And had he not been on a sea in that quiet,
Unthreatened moment and wasn't the Lord's power
There in his hand moving back and forth
In the small afternoon light, in his trying to find
The apposite word and pausing and staring dull-eyed?

He rose and walked down to the ocean and bent
Over the corpse and gently brushed his son's brow.
For a time he shook his head, back and forth,
Then rose and asked two men to bear "my child."

He trudged along a stony path, each step
A mimic to his stout dolorous heart.
No further words from Father Winthrop
Though the wind sighed for the vast cloud
That sometimes blocked the Lord's sustaining sky.

Guys

After work and over a beer, Steve Gazerko
Is describing the paternal black hole that is
The faint but genuine hair-shirt his soul
Wears each manly, holding-down-the-fort day.
What he's recalling is how his dad, Joe,
A mechanical engineer who went around
With one of those plastic pen and pencil carriers
In his shirt pocket, once asked his mother
How was it that love couldn't be fixed the way
Everything else could be fixed. This question
Was posed one night at the dinner table amid
The passing of Wonder Bread and Bluebonnet.
Steve's mother heaved an epical sigh, the sigh
Of generations of put upon women,
And answered that emotions weren't calculations.

"But," Steve goes on, "that's why guys are here—
To make things, break them and fix them." He opens
His hands and makes a sweeping gesture with his arms
As if to clear the air for revelation.
"Though I'll leave out the demiurge at the mainframe in the sky,
My dad was programmed—I mean put him
In a store filled with colored shirts and he'd choose a white one.
Give the man some screws, sprockets and pulleys
And he'd construct in no time a contraption
That would be a vision of frictionless efficiency."

"You mean," I say while idly fingering foam
On the glass rim, "the earth was never enough for him."
Steve regards me reflectively. "He was restless,
The way guys are restless, even when we're sitting tight
In a three-bedroom split-level, we're restless.
I mean look at that man-going-to-the-moon shit."

We both peer aimlessly into the blue-smoke room
Like animals whose confusion is their eloquence.

for David Cappella

My Great Aunt Gertie Who Lived to be Ninety-Eight

When I was a little girl
Growing up in Lanford,
I shot marbles with the boys
And sometimes when I knelt down
I dirtied the skirt of my dress.

My mother would scold me.
But do you know what an aggie is?
Have you ever read *King Lear*
By William Shakespeare?
Have you wandered on a heath
Or prairie or playground
When the sky is getting dark
And you are alone?

Where can I turn?
When I was a little girl
Growing up in a house
That had a big front porch
I used to sit on the steps
And razz the boys.

I had a tongue then
Before I got so old.
Have you ever read *King Lear?*
Our house was going to be torn down.
I was a little girl.

Where can I turn?
The king asks in *King Lear.*
He is out of his head with grief.
Once he was one of the boys
Who teased me for wanting
To shoot marbles.

I was good at it
And if I unclenched my hand
You could see the aggie
I am holding.
I need it, however.
I am on the heath.
The sky is dark. I am
A little girl. I hear many voices.
They want to leave me
But I won't let them.

On the Lawn of the Kinsman (1996, Frost Place, Franconia, NH)

A full moon in early August:
It sits amid the needling stars
Softly startling, a child's emblem
To admonish all sub-lunar
Beauties, to gild the dark.

The gathered poets sit
On the dewy lawn in the small hours
Exchanging tales of words,
Endurance and fitful powers.
For a northern night, it's warm

And the moonlight balm.
Longing forgets to fret
While their articulate pleasure
Winds above the crickets,
A lulling human music.

The pale light pulsates
With auras, murmurs rising
Into the quicksilver of second sight.
The tableau sings
Like the cold moon, a painted ring

Of frail eternity. The voices
Hum on. Make a wish—

But this would be that end
When love is near yet moonish,
When we accept our gifts.

Ductwork

Dave Mitchell doesn't see the picture in the newspaper
Of Abdul Munim Ali Hamood who is gesturing in a grimace
Of grief toward the corpse of his twenty-two-year-old son
Who was blown up by a lunatic in a car full of explosives.

It's not on the front page of the local paper, which has
A picture of a moose because the moose lottery was that day
And the right to legally shoot a moose is a big deal in Maine
Though who knows how many are poached for meat
Or shot for the evil hell of shooting something.

Dave doesn't read the paper anyway.
Words give him a headache and he's got enough
To think about what with driving his truck around
Delivering ductwork to contractors who are installing
Ventilation and heating systems in—you name it—
Restaurants, Laundromats, stores, garages, offices.

Probably when you're sitting and eating pork fried rice
You don't think about the ductwork and how the fans
Are blowing those hot oil fumes out into the night
But it's got to be there and Dave is good with it
Because it's steady work and he's married with a little girl
Though things have turned frosty between his wife and him.

They make love rarely and when they do it's over
Fast: two busy cogs, a narrow duty.
When Dave watches the women on the street

He craves them with a longing that goes beyond wishing.
He needs their bodies, needs to touch their nipples
And cup their breasts and break loose inside of them.

It's a bad feeling because he loved his wife
And doesn't know where that love went. Sure as shit
It's not in the daily with its headline moose story.
Dave used to hunt deer but doesn't do more now
Than keep his rifle clean and come winter sit
In an ice-fishing shack with some buddies, gab about
What happened to so-and-so and drink Jim Beam.

There are worse things, like pulling your back out the way
Rick Davis did at work last week or being a father
In Baghdad who has no twenty-two-year-old son anymore,
Who has nothing but the air to move his hands around in.

We can't live without that air, Dave knows that, and some days
When he's idling at a light and surrounded by spewing
Exhaust pipes he can imagine we'll ruin that. We'll get up
One morning, start gasping and turn blue. Right now, though,
It's lunchtime on the road, which means pulling the truck
Into Burger King and eyeing a woman in another line
And wondering what he'll do tonight when he gets home.
Maybe he'll finger the remote and see what's on.

Room (Manhattan, 1938)

Perhaps in another lifetime I already lived
In this room. I was a Gentile not a Jew.
I came to this busy island to make my fortune.
I wonder what happened in this little bare room.

In this life I stand at a window that looks out
On a painted brick wall touting soda pop,
A child's refreshment, though adults too drink it—
Some colored sugared water. I prefer black tea.

Though I stopped davening decades ago,
I am talking to God when I rehearse my diaspora—
The long history inside me, the hatred
Bequeathed me, the wary rabbinic eyes

Ever upon me. Here, I wear no badge.
I need not cower yet when I touch my face
I find no one. I am a disputation, smoke from
A cigarette, a ghost's cough. My ordeal winces—

The wish to have survival make me solid,
To span like cinema the rupture of continents.
I am, in fact, in purgatory—a sooty tenement,
A darkened hall, a closet that reeks of old clothes.

I read each advertisement duly,
The way an idiot would. In my own time

I am going to die. Such a solace to me!
Meanwhile, my soul buzzes like a housefly.

Meanwhile, I walk about this little room
And lower and raise the Venetian blinds.
The huge bottle stares back at me. It is as much
My friend as anything in this century.

Homage to Montale

This morning
The hummingbird's
Pure zigzag
Surprises you—
Its indifference to
The long steps
Of your mood.

The bellflowers hold
Open their careful mouths,
The wind booms softly,
Stone breathes in and out,
Millennia.

In various media
The Leader smiles as if
His teeth
Were a balm of sorts.
He repeats words
Carefully
As if lecturing
A class of children
Who pretend to be listening.

Aieee! Your head
Is full of human hurt.

Phrases will never
Anneal one
Scattered kiss of rain.
Always
You must walk
In the patrician light.

You raise your hands
Above your head
And birds stream
Through your cautious love.

Millenarians

When the Second Coming people stop by the house
And tell me that everything has to start over
That a new dispensation is at hand
I listen carefully

The strain of being fervently new each unblessed day
Of primping for newspaper columns
Broadcasts photographs glowing pixels
Is too much of a burden like having to
Be polite to the impolite
Tendering compliments to the woebegone
Finding hope amid mud and rubble

They do not speak to me as much as at me
But I do not blame them they see
That each person is a specimen
Another cloudy head
They are urgent and move their arms like marionettes
Time is not a permanent loan

If no one recognizes this besides a few
Millenarians in brown suits
And thickly polished shoes
It doesn't matter
There are many avant-gardes
They don't have to wander
Across stages assassinate texts
Install detritus in small white rooms

They don't have to be sardonic hip aggrieved edgy
They can be pleasant chat about
The weather dogs vinyl siding
They can live without the helpmate of irony

I take a number of these stapled
Prophecies that could ruin everyone's fun
I picture myself in an automobile on the way
To getting an oil change or buying natural food
Or sitting in an armchair and reading a biography
Of Rilke or doing the dishes
Who can say that moments form a necklace of eternity
Who can say that

We shake hands and I ask them
If they have heard of the poet William Butler Yeats
They are polite with me
One writes the name in a small spiral-bound pad
Who can say how poetry intersects God's trajectories
Who can say how the small "s" in spirit
Intersects with the capital "S" in Spirit

The Bible readers are dolefully puckish
Resolute
Thousands of ardent years
Thousands of calamitous years

Chet Baker

If glass could sing that would be Chet's voice
Toward the end that was there always because
Only the end intrigued him.
We were beginning and ending—each shared,
This-is-our-first-serious-relationship mood
Gyrating between passion and penance
So that after newspapers, TV, novels, sex, beer,
Stale pretzels and torrents of psychologizing talk
We lay listening in the dark to that voice
Soft and cold as February in a leafless park,
So sadly alive it seemed to beggar time.

When you love the sweetness of ruin,
Of the good going quietly bad and reveling
In torpor's pain, only the candy of heartache remains.
Like children we sucked on his brittle languor,
Lolled till dawn in that five-flights-up flat,
Waiting for a message we already had received.

Contretemps

Was I too soon?
Was I unclear?
Was it my voice?
Was it my stare?

I looked away
And hid a smile.
I twitched with fear.
I scared my wiles.

You looked askance.
You were perturbed.
You sat down hard.
You barely heard.

The sky caught fire.
The moon hung close.
The wind backed off.
The flowers froze.

When time resumed,
I closed a door.
Love sang its song
From a far shore.

Annisquam

Some contractor in the 20s' idea of colonial America—
   Low ceilings, timbers, fireplaces,
Dark inside because of the tiny windows—
     But she loved it
Which meant only one Cape Codder at cocktail hour,
    The predictable rush
 Of alcohol tuning her spirit at the end
  Of a not disagreeable day, offering
A little unearned increment.

          This was back
  When women didn't necessarily work a job in the world
   And she was home doing laundry,
    Cleaning and cooking but
     Reading books too—novels—or sitting at the table
In the breakfast nook and writing letters to her sister
     In Saint Louis.

The house was a haven
     And sometimes she'd lie in bed at night and talk
With Bill about the birds,
How the wind was blowing hard off the ocean
     And what it was like
 For the birds who were out there in the cold and dark.

Sometimes she even cried about it.
It sounds a bit crazy, a grown woman,
But it's what I mean by her being happy,

That her feelings
Didn't end with her own body,
That the house was a skin and the sky
Was a skin and all the skins were open
To one another like lovers,
Like strength and frailty.

It made her cry
Sometimes because she'd lost her fear of sadness.
No longer was she a character in Chapter Seven
Where the skirt-chasing evangelist trumpets his
Vain innocence
Or the heroine is diced up by a boat propeller.

She didn't need a mundanely bitter ending.
The false heights of melodrama didn't have to leer
Precipitously.

She was free to walk
From room to room and pause to look out
A window
At the clouds drifting across the sky
And forget the weary intelligence of identity.

Attic

God runs the dogs,
Hansen of Ward Six would say
A few hundred times a day.
No fog

In his attic. He crackled like
Between-stations static.
He'd been vicious, a quick
Barroom knife.

That was endless pills ago.
Rookies asked old-timers
What he meant. They mimed
A grin or shrugged. *Slow*

Train that never came
Yet each urgent time
He spoke anew. A synapse chimes
Late and for decades

Pneuma gnashes
And sizzles, the plaything
Of Sophoclean suffering.
Chickadees on the ash

Trees some well-meaning arborist
Planted in the prior century

Darted skittishly.
A nervous fist

Greeted a sweaty palm.
The mind is shame's grimace,
Is anger-lava, is
Calm

As an old dog lying
In a sunny red clay yard.
And God hoards the hard
Note mercy cannot sing.

Shakespeare in Mud

How pathetic
He was, too busy even to steep himself
In the beery companionable fumes of pity.
A free man but bound to step briskly into
The streets of turds and straw and march himself
Off to rehearsals, pleas, wrangles
Or the spleen of players' hung-over wit.
One more pun on will and he'd kill someone.

Beyond his conjuring reach
Real princes clamored, fought and wenched
While he set his trenchant fancy to speeches,
Speeches, speeches.

How had he come
To spend his green life in the cradle of language,
How had he come to this cool bath
In the parboiled souls of others?
Sometimes, he flinched to see his own fingers,
Feel his thinning hair, touch his lips.

Words dwarfed the humors that prompted them:
A conceit requisite for authoring,
A winking lie, a candle of raveled time.

And yet when striding in the strength of his meter,
When a voice was speaking to and through him
That made each daily word dull banter,

He wished the great witless world might know
That praise and dispraise were wind to him,
That his love was iron, gossamer, blood and honey,
That he was the man who cut through death's costumes,
Who traced the pliant veins of self-deceit
Like a palm-reading gypsy, who confessed
The passion of the disabused, who, hopeless and candid,
Kissed the weltering star of calamity.

He looked down.
Dung and dirt. They too spoke. And he heard.

The Pump

Drawing water, three short down-strokes
   on the pitcher pump inside the house,
   five staunch clanging down-strokes
   on the long-neck pump outside,
   gush.

Carrying water in a bucket carefully
   so as not to spill.

Striking a match to light the kindling scraps,
   the first flame blue and soft.

Filling the lamps with kerosene,
   feeling darkness coming so gently.

Washing hands in a metal basin.

Bringing in firewood, the weight of the logs
   seeming to drive the body forward.

Sitting on the back porch,
   watching wind ruffle aspen leaves.

Day and night were dust settling on a shelf,
   dreamlessly content.

Sometimes when I stepped outside I thought
  I might meet pilgrims—
  souls who were still on foot.

I would shake their weathered hands, hear
  their searching words, offer them bread
  baked in the cook stove, stroll a ways
  together down our narrow road.

Nothing but time's stern breathing,
  stars we see and do not see,
  stony earth steadying our pensive feet.

Nothing but the pump and the water
  that we took into our bodies,
  that fell through our cupped hands,
  that spoke for a cold sublimity.

Bax

Frayed—and not only around his

Weary eyes but in his once staunch
Soul-nucleus—Bax wonders
If I've started his elegy yet.

I tell him I don't go in
For that line of goods until
The proper season arrives.

He tells me that's one reason
I'm bad with money. "The winter trade
Show is in June. Everyone knows that

Except you. You think that riding
The moments is genius. Ech."
Bax mumbles, spits and coughs.

I reach over to caress his cheek,
Feel the lean beard and creases
That run from his mouth to

Deep within the grieving earth.
Bax knows what I'm thinking
And shrills a few strangled notes

Of opera—dull death
Mocked by brisk life. Bax giggles—
A worn-out sepia wheeze.

Brown eyes glister with pain:
"No lie, I fucked up big-time."
Both moody this near the abyss

We let the words subside.
My left hand grips his right
Like science clutching a penny.

My Last Borders, or Poem Ending with a Homage to W. B. Yeats

Once I read in a Borders Bookstore
In a sea of shopping malls in New Jersey.
A man sat in the first row and pawed over
The poems he was going to read later during the open mic.
He never looked up at me but snorted occasionally
With vatic delight at his own precipitous genius.
The espresso machine in the rear of the café
Made troubled basso sounds like a dying cow.

I read in the café because the "events area"
Was hosting a talk on "Planning a Trust Fund."
My books for sale were under a table on which a slide
Projector sat and showed screens like "Your House—
Your Greatest Asset" and "Tomorrow Does Come."

A woman in the third row (there were only three rows)
Talked intermittently on a cell phone to someone named Yvette:
"Are you really staying in a hotel, Yvette?"
"You can get that much cheaper in Paramus."
"I can't believe you're still seeing that loser."
When people told her to be quiet, she said
That she liked to talk and listen to poetry
At the same time. She said she was "multi-sensory."
After the reading she came up to me and told me
She thought I was going to be a hick from Maine
But I turned out to be a Jewish intellectual.

She informed me that she was Jewish too, that novelists were smarter
Than poets and that she had been to Europe eight times.
After the events director crawled under the Trust
Planning Table and brought my latest title back to the café,
She bought one of the two books that were sold that evening.

How sad am I to do these readings?
Just normal-aching-poet-sad?
Delmore-Schwartz-cornered-by-the-abyss sad?
Or cowardly? Afraid to be Sylvia-Plath-angry-sad
And barge through death's sullen door,
Sick of human idiocy, including my own?

Later in the evening when I have repaired
To the poetry section to gather my slender wits,
I consult the oracle Yeats.
He never drove on Interstates among convoys of 18-wheelers,
Never searched asphalt acres for a parking space
Around Christmas, never took a self-assertion seminar
Or credit management workshop in a fluorescent warehouse.
The chains of commerce never danced for him.

He stood for the soul's exactions, the flawed
Avid beauty of conscience. I read his poems
And feel better, which is to say, sadder.

Wisdom

She didn't like him: long nose hairs,
Voice patient yet overbearing (a voice
Meant for a world of women-as-children).
He'd expect a yielding kiss if not more.

She repaired to the ladies room pleading
The time of month. It wasn't and she'd have
To leave some hour but by then he'd be history.
He'd tell his buddies that he'd ditched her.

The road to joy was never paved with bliss.
She sat in a stall and pulled a pocket
Tao Te Ching from her purse. The Way eluded her.
That must be why it was so ancient.

Women came and went, came and went,
Talking of relationships. To whom could she
Petition for sexual asylum? Later,
In the violet dusk, she clutched her empty book.

Smoking in Midtown

I want to say it's all women
But there are men too though it seems most of the time
It's women who stand out in the weather in front
Of tall buildings and smoke cigarettes.

Sometimes only one person
Is there, a "solitary figure," as poems used to say in the era
When a standard emotional image was no disgrace to drop into
The collection box, but however many people there are, they seem
In their abstracted poses as they brush a crumb off a lapel
Or shift their feet, to be the only people in America who dare
To be seen thinking in public. You can watch the thoughts
    betraying
Their faces: what I am going to say to her, what he said to me,
How much the checking account is overdrawn, the brakes on
The SUV still are too tight and on and on into supra-
Idealist wastelands of uneasiness, to say nothing of random
Pangs about sex.

You couldn't build a building big
Enough to house all the thoughts of the smokers in midtown.
Mental energy is an impossible force based in a frail venue,
Which leads to the introduction of mortality into the poem
    because these
Sources of life, generatrixes and priestesses of the breeding
    emotion,
The very roses of blood, are sucking on what their kids who have

Been exposed to a health-conscious, moralizing, elementary school
Curriculum refer to as "death sticks."
                    You don't have to have a Ph.D.
In sociology to know that women do not get the respect due them,
That the buildings and the money that made the buildings were
        the work
Of men who then went home to the little woman or the
        dipsomaniac woman
Or the angry-but-not-showing-it-until-the-guy-opens-his-self-
        important-mouth
Woman, but smoking is pleasant in its garish harsh way,
The anxious inhale and then blowing the smoke out. That's a
        semi-
Sublime second or two right there.

                    Plus there's gossiping if someone
Familiar is present or complaining or talking about what an idiot
        someone
Else is. Men and women can both be idiots; it's gender-blind,
But as I said, a lot of times the smoking is solo and has an I-got-to-go-
Down-to-the-street quality and the woman's hand is shaky.

                    Mental pain is worse than dislocating
Your finger or a sinus infection because it goes on and on and
Setting it right may be another delusion that brings more pain.

                    This woman is thinking hard and the city could
Sink beneath her thoughts as in some Hollywood urban horror
Epic except there's no hunky guy with an automatic weapon and
Nuclear biceps to make things right. Instead, there is this woman

Who has on a white blouse with a small but noticeable tomato
Stain at the waist. The collar of the blouse is frilly; her hair is
     teased-up
Medium-high. Her eyes are gaunt. When another woman comes out
The revolving door and lights up, she turns to her and gives her
The biggest, most beautiful smile of cognizance—you, my puffing
     sister.

Crawford, Nebraska

March 25th. Driving at night
Through western Nebraska we are suspended
In the cushioned quiet of a wet spring snow—
Nickel-sized flakes plummeting deliberately.
No wizard of enchantment or Caesar or king
Or khan could have commanded such a pure spectacle.
The inky sky is a heaven and in no hurry.

We park and start to walk through a little town
Whose name we read on the post-office lintel.
It's late and still and the windows are mostly dark.
The innocence of sleep is palpable.
You say that small towns are like elegies,
That they bring up the sharpest feelings of frailty.

We walk past snowy cottonwood trees
And street signs and pickup trucks. The snow will vanish
By late morning and so will we. We stop in the middle
Of a sidewalk and stick our tongues out and taste
The cold sky, the houses, the low calm breathing
Of children and men and women, the teeming
Wordless drift that subdues everything.

From *The White Words* (1983)

Passing Significance

"No one of importance here," the chief assessor
Mutters as he stamps the snow off his boots
And looks around at his fellow travelers
In the sitting room of an inn
That is the only inn thereabouts.

No one picks up his remark.
The young man in the shadows
In the far corner continues to think about
The letter he should write. Occasionally, he takes
A gold watch from his coat pocket and toys with it
Absent-mindedly. An infant cries.
A woman sings softly,
A border song about flowers and stars.
In front of the fireplace sit two nuns.
The innkeeper's wife keeps sneezing.
She wonders who will try to sneak off
Without paying. A dog, at the feet
Of an old man with huge mustaches, sighs.
A clerk contentedly rustles
What passes for a newspaper in these parts.

There are names for everyone, for every day
And every sort of weather. There are kings
On top of promulgating kings. To study other people
You must be free and easy and remember nothing.

Then you will see what it is about each one of them
That has passing significance. There is a book somewhere.
In it are names, as beautiful as they are obscure.

Of Small Towns

It is not so much gossip that absorbs
Them as a fondness, to be found
Even in the children, for measuring lives:
The noting of how many years some wife
Has outlived her husband and how each of the road
Commissioner's four children quit high school
In the middle of the eleventh grade and how
It was twenty years to the day (they are
All addicted to anniversaries) that
A black spruce fell on a one-armed man.
Comparison is insistent—the father who
Is a better shot but not as good a card
Player as the son; the sister who
Writes poems while the other two clean house.
Here, people want to live to learn
Who the next President will be, how many
Games the World Series will go,
Whether the trains will ever come back.
Ceremonious and dutiful to national symbols,
Too many of the sons die in the wars.
The coffins show that faraway places exist,
That you can die quite forcibly elsewhere.
Those who have hoisted themselves up
And fled will say that the finitude
Of small-town life breeds idiocy, that
The imagination turns upon itself, chews
Its substance over and over until it is worse
Than nothing. The surmises that the metropolis loves

To make, the crushes of people whose names you will
Never know, the expansive gestures made
Among incoherent buildings—all that is
Peculiarly urban and self-aware is lacking.
Instead, you have a hodgepodge:
Legends hovering, dreams that lapse into manias,
Characters ransacked like cottages in winter.
Each random movement would become an event.
It is no surprise that every now and then
The attentiveness becomes too great
And some hamlet spawns a horror
Of the first degree. As is to be expected,
The *émancipé*'s letters home are blunt:
"You are all like those vile canning jars,
Lidded and sealed and put away for endless winter."
And yet—it is these towns that dignify the slimmest
Of lives with a history, remembering even dogs
With an earnest pleasure, a rush of anecdote and regret.

A History of Photography

Prodigies flooded the market—the magnetic corset,
The one-twist tooth extractor, the camera.
At the exhibitions only the occasional
Yokel, up from the South, gaped in disbelief.

The Church was not in principle opposed
To such an invention. Baudelaire granted its
Historical worth. Now, great-grandparents
Could be scrutinized, lost courtyards found.

Reality, the dumb beast, yawned.
A few ocular spirits became
Photographers, another semi-profession,
Self-employed and self-taught. "I am not

A mechanic!" they yipped petulantly.
You saw them with their apparatuses
Roaming quays, moors, poor quarters,
Parliaments. There could be, the wits

Explained, no events without photographers.
Still, who could argue with modern life?
And for every megalith machine
Relief could be found in a dewy flower,

A battered hat, a frolicsome roué.
Possessed by moments, photographers

Appeared immune to time's lengthier taunts.
Like warm-tongued cats, they gladly lapped

From the brimming, giddy saucer of sight.
Walls held their visions comfortably.
Mom smiled, Dad winked, the camera whose
Omniscience the reviewers found "refreshing" blinked.

Letter from New England

"Poor deity," murmured one of the mourners, "ever shuffling
And dealing from the same pack of cards."

A typical mid-winter day,
Mirthless sun giving way to gray sky
And minute dry snow.
                              The hearse halted
For two dogs sparring in the street.

No one dared separate them.
                              They staggered off finally,
Exhausted and whimpering.
                              A woman—someone said
A cousin—began to laugh almost haughtily.

At what who knows?
                    Perhaps the blood
On immaculate snow.

An elder conveyed her down a side street.

Directly above the minister's head on a limb of an elm
A cardinal perched, then flew off after rapt seconds.

My daughter plans to write a sonnet
About it.
              The young may be forgiven, I suppose,

Their craving for the emblematic.
                              For me,
The boosting of the image has always signaled
A grasping expedient wit.

The Brothers

In the lives I liked to read as a boy there were always
Two brothers. One knew what to make of things.
His mind was full of gears. His hands were clever.
He saved up to visit the Exposition. Adults praised him.
The other brother loved horses, made up stories
And went around barefoot. He died of whooping cough
Or influenza at age eleven. It was sad but it
Was all right because he would not have become Someone.
He didn't want anything to differ
From what it was. He was complete already.

I could imagine his large milky eyes
And wavering voice. His brother, the one who lived
And became famous, teased him. Of course, he took it
Good-naturedly. That was how he was, good-natured.
In the books, the locales and hardships varied but
The brothers were constant. It seemed to have
To be that way, with one having ideas
And saying, "Can't you see?" and the other spending
Afternoons in the hayloft watching swallows.
It was the romance of common sense
I was reading, the new galvanic industrial
Fairy tale. I still think of them and how rivers
Divide nations, how nothing precious can be measured,
How one brother seizes the sluggish day,
While the other is smote and lost.

Piano Lessons

"The Johnsons have her and so must we":
That is how I came to know Miss Lee.
I was to play the piano, if not well
Then enough so that my mother could tell
Another mother I was taking again this year—
It was an expense, but I was a dear.

Miss Lee would coax me and I would cry.
"I can't do any better however I try;
It isn't in me," I'd wail, then steel myself once more.
Miss Lee would motion and start to pace the floor
And we were off again, manacled to one
Another by our common sense of misfortune.

I knew it was harder for her than for me:
She had to watch while I defiled what she esteemed.
At night she played for herself alone;
But even then the music was not her own,
For the neighbor boys would gather on her walk
And at some bravura passage begin to squawk,
Crow, shout, huzzah, yelp, bray,
Till she came out on her porch and they ran away.

Her talent, the town observed, kept her poor.
Once, she cursed me, another time she slammed a door
And ran upstairs. I heard her rolling on her bed.
When she came down, she smiled sadly and said,
"That's enough for today." Next week came.

72

I loitered outside until she called my name,
Then shuffled in. "Someday you will be great,"
She said, and I felt she was talking straight
Past me and into another world where
There were no clumsy fingers nor fidgety glares
At the clock on the wall nor hectoring half-notes
Nor folded dollar bills. I took off my coat,
And we walked into the room where the piano stood
For all that we wanted to do yet never would.

The Light Child

This tender certainty sits lightly as
A good king's mantle. Like calls to like:
The circle of marbles, the balsa plane
That soars ten feet and descends to earth,
The cocoon on the garden fence. What is learned
Is what wants to be learned, is bidden
By the leaping mind. Fascination is homely,
Pockets are to be filled and exclamations
Actual. Even the tears that disrupt
A moment are proper, showing as they do
That no shield intrudes between alacrity
And rough matter. A fall is a fall—a bemoaned
Yet soon diminished fact, a misstep amid
Untamed abundance. Eternities dawdle;
There is much to purely do. His day is a dawn.

for Owen

Some Happiness

I tell my daughter about this pitfall
And that difficulty.
She listens, but it is hard
For her to be patient.
With a kiss, I dismiss her
And she dismisses me.

She is happy. I pick at that
Commonly discredited fact.
It is something I had not thought of,
That love might have this humming, incautious outcome,
That a daughter could be like the sea
In the rain, absorbing the many drops.

She is
All things that steadily, waveringly go.

I am on the shore, kicking at what I know.

There is a day without conclusions.
There is a word without weight.
There is an impulse familiar as skin.

I lay my perils down.
Childhood is a string tied
To a great, remarkable nothing.

We dance
To a music beyond misgiving.

for Maisie

The White Words

Words, it turned out, were
White but not to be contemned.
The streets of Baltimore, the novels
Of Trollope, the future of my sister:
All topics contained the lulling rhythm
That was talk, wave upon graceful
And laborious wave. For a time the toil
Of pain would disperse. In my mother's eyes
A startled serenity would appear. Morphine
Was forgotten, and I wanted to a wooden
Thing, a half-human marionette capable
Of talking forever, a brave body hoping
To coax from that puffy blotched face
A smile, however bewildered and slow:
Applaud life.
        I wore down,
My tongue became heavy and thick.
The very air seemed sickly.
Two tired strangers, we looked about
Distractedly for that spot where
The white words still hovered.

Cord of Birch

It was high summer, that time when winter seems
Implausible, a moralist's admonitory dream,
That I, short-sleeved, took through the neighborhood
A question, revealing it only when it was understood
All round that the amenities as to heat and flies
Had been upheld, when something like response might thrive.
A hundred-sixty years of working in the woods,
Their lives were sure to hold the fact or two
I wanted about some birch I'd cut that spring
And its aptitude for producing heat.
To a man they grunted—to let me know they knew
That I was bothering about a very poor thing.
I relaxed in the shade of their attitude,
Ignorant that each was to recall, surmise, delete
And aver that which the others had said was untrue.
Gravely I agreed with their unblinking contrarieties.
My hand shook hands and the doubt inside me
Hurrahed. Back home the cord loitered, a pile
I'd left beside the back path. I pouted awhile,
Hefted a piece—wood. No surety descended.
At night in bed I defined, mused and pretended;
Nothing came of it but dismal sleep.
By New Year's the snow was over two feet deep;
Load by load my dilemma was taken away,
And often I paused to stare on the way
Back from the shed at the smoke the fire had freed,
Almost enraptured by the wisdom of need.

Immigrant's Letter

Everyone thinks they know what it is like here.
The ones who were born here know because they have
Always been here. It is their home and they can tell
When something is out of place. The ones who came here
Know because they have had to learn everything. Study
Has made them practiced observers. I, however,
Know nothing of this place. In this I do not mean to scold
Or play the fool. It is true that I did not know what
I was getting into, but I knew what I was leaving.
Work for nothing back there—die like a plow horse.
I knew what I was leaving. Here you can sit
All day and no one says anything to you about it.
It is assumed that you are thinking. It is a courtesy
I appreciate, but they are such an unelaborate people.
It is like a big, easy-going army. Is that it?
Everyone gives himself a task. There is a sort of general
In a business suit at the top. He smiles but is stern.
All you have to do is want what everyone else wants,
And you belong here. It does not matter how much
You possess—you would not believe what "rich" means here—
It is the wanting that helps everyone get along.
Even when you get old and die, you still want.
It is like a parade. What I would not give for one
Of their cars! I would do nothing but drive.
My ass would get soft; my fingers would make love
To the steering wheel. What I do have are sunglasses.

You cannot see me in them: I become like a fish
In water or a magician. I am sending no
Money home this letter. I know nothing.

The Spirit That Speaks

The spirit that speaks in the iris
Exclaiming at length a poise of blossom
Is not spirit but laborious congruence,
A slow stiff dance, words raining on
The loam of actions, the shy shop girl
Falling in love with a handsome stranger,
Evolution as passion.

A credulous event, never an answer,
With no goal unless repetition were a goal,
Feet moving because they were feet,
Possibility like a child leery of water
Waddling eon-slow toward the edge
Of the pond of being.

           Remove the iris and the world
Goes, a zeppelin ripped and plummeting,
The industrious captains peering out
The widening portholes, wondering for the first time,
As birds and baggage fly by, if
Existence is, after all, a passive tumult,
An unprincipled verb, a blind man's certainty.

All this, and more, the iris would not tell me.

From *Good Trembling* (1985)

Friday Night

Dinner winds down and the bottom
Of the accompanying bottle appears
With the abruptness of a smile
Or plainclothesman's badge. The people
Are friends, the moments idle as jewels.
Though not written in any constitution or
Call to arms, this congress occurs everywhere.
Praise to convivial gossip!
Praise to the flesh of broiled fish
Doused with lemon and thyme!
Praise to the ardor that scintillates
In idioms and cigarettes!

The hostess hunches over the table,
Wags her head, speaks rapidly.
The host flips an apple from hand to hand.
Everyone has survived a week's panics.
Everyone offers testimony: cars that
Stopped moving, jokes, head colds, hope.
Myths are not dead. This is the table
Of life—one and many, ripe
With the canny scent of brandy,
Worth the hospitable journey.

Stitches

On a table in the front yard of a house
By the highway selling "odds 'n' ends"
Is something not made on any day shift—
Handkerchiefs embroidered with flowers,
Hearts, quarter moons, houses, ducks.

They are not beautiful, but they are pretty
And better than anything they are someone's
Precious time—be it by a window or in
A little attic room or on a veranda—they
Are someone's time, which you can see
In each tiny stitch that is too small to see
But is there the way the funny yellow ducks
Are there or the purplish five-petal flowers.

I pay two dollars for the lot of them,
This quiet work that did not have to be done.

Each moment in them is straight and steady and
You can see that a hand is a body
And a body is a life and a life is
The habit of time and seems, to someone who
Happens by later like this, the remainder of design.

Elvis Presley

Charlene, the oldest of your sisters,
Looks into her tequila twister
And somberly relates
To you and me and the cat and the egg-smeared plates
The accidental suicide of the king.
No one could do a thing
About it because the pauper had become a prince.
No one has known what to do since.
We go upstairs to get away from her
Lugubrious lewdness, but as we murmur
And groan I can hear the music downstairs,
A thick rising honey.
                             You say you don't care
About me anymore. I reflect
That society is the time between sex.
There's a lurch, clatter and weak shout.
I step over Charlene on the way out.
You have these Elvis dreams.
There is no time in-between.

Soap Opera

If each witless age fondles an image of itself,
Ours is a woman crying for help
Amid a crowd of well-coifed friends.
She is hysterical, tormented, saddened, upset.
In a few minutes she will be better

And stay that way till she desponds again.
It was nothing that made her cry.
Ralph told Joan that Bill might die.
Wistfully she floats through the harsh light
That bounces off linoleum and glass.

She is crying again and has locked the door.
Dressed for middling success
She is not ugly or stupid or poor
But her feeling for feelings persists.
Like a sleep-deprived detective

She lurches through the alibis of affairs
And good-byes, the dry rot of truth,
Varicose recrimination.
She opens the door.
Tom ogles her and smiles.

They kiss. It might be pretense,
Tenderness or lustful urge.
Adroit music surges over throw rugs

And well-waxed floor. We are convinced.
Happiness is the best of styles.

Annuals

Grays, browns, mottled blacks:
Whether withered, frost-attacked
Or simply deceased, all annuals
Go into this heap from which
Others will derive
Increase.

Death has its small uses,
And you, my wife and a gardener,
Are respectful and sensibly sad.
The commands of the seed
Contained no surprise, yet
We oohed and ahhed as if
Each bloom were somehow
Unforeseen.

Though lovingly saluted
Beauty will not be known.
The purposing bee explains nothing.
These stringy petals and
Brittle leaves bequeath no aesthetic
Moralities.

Crumble of earth and stems—
We minister to each other.
The blossom of a memory
Succumbs to its vigor but
Will revive (you say) another

Summer, displaying the calm
Insouciance of what never went
Away.

for Janet

The Oxymoron as Taoist Vision

I do not call something "wisdom"
When I can predict the next verity.
Because we use the same words
Does not mean we have the same eyes.
A strange bird flew through the village this morning.

People said it was a chaffinch, an egret, a falcon.
One old man swore it was a magpie.
What a blessing disappearance is!
The bird goes its way and the people
Chatter their eager heads off.

I like surprises, minglings, distances, leaps,
The inveterate magic of "bitter" and "sweet,"
The humility of "failure."
Some child is laughing at a bowl of cereal.
Some cloud does not know it is a cloud.

Some fat moment has begun to diet.
If you are skillful,
Each sullen fact becomes incongruous.
Even the "progress" the mayor brags about
Will begin to sing and smirk and after a time

Spew bubbly admissions—eras
Spent dallying amid the soft shores

And comfy cabanas of unimproved joy.
I clap my hands
And they sound like mountains dancing.

Stock Car Racing

It makes me nervous to think about it,
Which is why I'm here.
Looking subdues me
And these other folks who are present
On a sunny southern Sunday afternoon—
Post-church, post-hangover or both.

                        The drivers dress
Like astronauts and used to be poor.

                        The guy
Behind me won't shut up about Jesus.
"This clamor is science," Russ, my literate confederate,
Proclaims and hoists his Bud in a gesture meant
To bless the metal choir of revving flatheads.
These pre-Apocalyptic days a vocab erupts
For each technical hiccup.

                        Driving nowhere for
The sake of driving seems poetic,
Though logos blanket each automotive inch.
Through my binoculars I observe Miss
Winston waving and displaying a winningly
Goat-like grin.

                        My jaw aches while I try to imagine
What it's like to be calm and tense
At the same time except I'm not hurtling
Round and round at a hundred sixty miles
Per hour and am glad of it.

                        How do they

Prepare themselves?
                        Now the Jesus freak
Is lamenting the flaming death of Junior Babcock.
The infernal noise seems louder.
A yellow Pontiac spins
Coming out of a curve and you
Can feel everybody's fear at something
Unwanted
Yet exciting occurring.
                        Just like
That the driver regains control, and no one
On the track or in the stands has
Even paused; yet we have considered the impact
Of possibility and needled by that
Knowledge we have been reborn.

John Milton Goes Flying

The earth sped away. Villages and steeples
Grew "insignificant"—the flight instructor's
Routine dismissal sieved through a thin smile.
His nodding student squinted like a jeweler,
Shook his bewigged head in baffled wonderment.
The sun dazzled, the motor stuttered
Some potent yet arcane Greek phrase.

So prayer at last took metal form—
The sort of soaring one would expect of man
Who when faced with heaven and light,
The golden sheen of unclouded grace,
Puttered, picked up an appropriate tool,
Said something uplifting but trite.

Good Trembling

"Good trembling," CJ announced as we
Prowled the docksides in our careless jackets.
The unrepentant winter scowled.

Metaphysical toughs, we broadcast
Expressive urges to any unwilling
Populace. A cartoon balloon

Of herbal insight hovered over us.
"I don't want to become a statement," I stated
While shuddering at the prospect

Of comfort—thirty-five and married.
A cop car slowed down beside us—longhairs.
"I can't grok that," CJ said. "Man,

It's blow-your-head-off windy out here."
The large indifferent Ford motored on,
A capsule of warmth and congealed opinion.

We sat in an all-night with some coffee,
Exchanged barrages of quotations,
Promised to redeem the inertia

Of everyone else and went out
Once more into that portent wind
Of dogmas, vows and the thinnest smoke.

The Suicide's Father

Everything has become a museum.
Where I live is where I lived.
My face in the mirror in the morning
Was my face. I am here the way a chair
Or painting is here. I have weight and
A meaning I cannot possess.

We walked to the war plaza, bought bags
Of popcorn, watched the jugglers and mimes,
Walked home through the lamp-lit twilight.
It was a Sunday in early spring.

What do you do when the past is
No longer yours? I was a simple man.
I thought it was something that could not
Be taken away. I would have it
For always.

In those stances, excursions, mornings—
Even in laughter—I see death.
It is wrong but that is what I see.

I have put my purposes in a burlap bag
And thrown them in the river and watched
Them sink. It did not take long.
It is cold in that river and now when I walk
I wander like a tramp or bored pensioner.
People avoid me or banter courteously.

You, my boy, are never mentioned.
That is for the best. I have
Committed a crime but am not sure
What it was. It is a crime where there
Are no police or reports or even lies.
It is a crime of meals, presents,
Postcards, worries, lullabies.

There was the time you asked for money,
The time I didn't hear from you for months.
But we have those times and live.
We come around. We walk through a door
Into the right, welcoming room.

You did not like illusions.
You did not like those grimacing mimes.
They baffled words yet
I spoke gladly concerning you:
My son this, my son that.
My son built little, wooden airplanes
That really flew. I was proud. Like the mime who
Could not open an imagined door, you frowned.

You were in the river for days
Before they found what they said was you.
I had to say it too.
On what was a hand was a ring.

What was there before this
To think twice about? Everything.
Everything.

Essay: The Hudson River School

You see it particularly in paintings of
The mid-nineteenth century—that serene, beckoning distance,
As if they could not look too closely at what was near
Preferring instead the vista of endless promise
For which the nation became famous.
It wasn't those clichéd, too-contented,
Pastoral afternoons—the air rich with drowsy chaff—
Nor those educated bows to Poussin and Claude
That made the reviewers boast and declaim.
It was as acolytes of natural sentiment
And limners of momentous terrain that such painters
Were determinedly American.
                              Even amid
Patriot brags, there are particulars with which
A viewer must reckon. Though, for instance,
The figures in their pictures are often dwarf-small,
They do not seem humbled. They labor intently
Or from an overlook gaze at the lucent enormity
Spread before them. Here the mind will live
Fully. Here will dwell a country of sensible
Yet inspired citizens. Politics will not lack eyes.

In the middle ground sits a series of perfect planes
Whose grandeur is a fable of equilibrium.
The mountains are staunch as deacons.
A lake lies limp as a cloth.
Each tree is the image of a tree.
We behold the forest of an Edenic patrimony

100

Where we cannot live—it is the distance—
But cherish as a moral charm.

There is a further distance, which although aerial
Avoids heaven. Sensation is uncertain,
But such unclouded prospects comfort
And gently speculate. Remoteness means no harm;
These are landscapes of a thorough mercy,
An ambient grace.

The Mowing Crew

The mourners drive away
And talk about the graves.

Old man Shorey can't
Keep the mowing boys at work.
They take off
Their shirts and lie in the sun
Beside their machines
And go to sleep.

Young as they
Are, the grass doesn't bother them.
Their hair is girl-long.
They smile and spit.

Even when one of their own
Dies with his car on
The state highway, they don't
Seem to exactly believe it.

Standing at the graveside
They look placidly
At the dark riven ground
And nod to each other
As if it were another
Hot day and they felt
Drowsy and wished to lie down.

Europe (1893)

Again and again in the dusty, twilit parlor
Memory summoned its cultured palette.
Amid oils of swains and kings, *objets d'art*
And Roman appurtenances never seen

In a Massachusetts hill town,
One tried to grasp the pure, reducible thing,
The preference that had no local correlative,
That breathed a nobler yet wistful air.

The voyagers intoned heuristic thoughts—
Comparisons and questions more often than not:
What did one make of Bernini, Van Eyck, the Ring?
What was there about a Tuscan spring?

Snow dripped from the eaves in lackadaisical drops
While the guest, a pilgrim of sorts, ahem-ed
Avowals about the world-at-large—
Contessas, villas and cyclamens.

Wise looks competed with the cream and tea.
Who wanted to live and die without
Having sampled the froth of refinement?
And what was the point of this endless, obscure

Making? When would America be done?
Each day went by undefined in a town about

Which, because it was American, one could
Say only it was like any other town.

One wanted repose, insight, beauty, wit.
Instead, one made these visits and listened as
Each apt word betrayed the paucity
Of time and place. Eternity might

Have wept for this blunted passion. One day
At the stable Gaffer Smith asked what it mattered
What such people thought? Wasn't the Pope a dago?
From their second floor they could see the *campagna*

As if it were yesterday. The unstartled heat
Of New England's August seared the placid dust.
In the front hall beside Dante's bust
Civilization said goodbye. Later, on the way

Down Elm Street, other meanings seemed meant.
The untutored night intimated a continent.

for Sydney Lea

The Fall of the Human Empire

When a dog is struck by a car.
A civilization collapses. A bystander
Explains this absence of allegory
As the dog whines about its accidental pain,
Wobbles and lurches. It is a gray afternoon
In the city. This shorthaired mongrel
Is not a bomb or a lie.
Two cars stop and a student on the way home
From the public library reflects on how
Chekhov could see the world through the eyes
Of a dog. "No one believes me"—
Such is the miserable thought that is
The sonata of these confusions. Clarity
Is equivalent to pain in this world.
Even a writhing dog, who is not Chekhov,
Could tell you that. There needs to be
An official for this compromising situation.
There needs to be an economy.
Dogs are like habits. This one sobs
And tries to drag itself elsewhere.
In operas people sing with all their hearts
About a missing love letter or a shoe.
The world cannot be quiet any longer
About this dog. The peril is too great.
Silence is a dictator who lets you live
Today so you can be murdered tomorrow.
Don't fool yourself.
This dog is as peerless as you.

I Try to Explain to My Children a Newspaper Article Which Says That According to a Computer a Nuclear War is Likely to Occur in the Next Twenty Years

Death (I say) used to have
Two faces: one good, one bad.
The good death didn't like to do it—
Kill people, dogs, insects, flowers—
But had to. It was his duty.
He would rather have been playing cards—
Crowing over an ace or shrugging at a deuce.
Without him the earth would get too crowded,
The soil would become weary, feuds would
Overtake love. That was what death
Believed—and when we thought about it
We agreed.
        The bad death was a bully.
He would kill angels if he could.
He settled for children, poets—
And I say some strange names to them:
Osip Mandelstam and *Federico García Lorca*—
All flesh increased by spirit.
He bragged, made wagers and said
Mean things about the human race.
People, he said, made his job easy.
They were full of confusion that
Soon became hatred. *Tsk, tsk,* he would
Chide as if in sympathy.

The nations of the world offered him
Their love.
             The new death doesn't
Have a face. He is
Calm, distant, devoted, thorough.
Though he makes a show of reason,
He is crazy. The other two deaths
Do not like him, the way he wears
A tie as if death were an office,
The way he wants to be efficient.
How smug he is! Fate and fortune
Bore him. There cannot be enough death,
He says. He points with pride at his theorems.
You will put us out of business,
The other two complain but he doesn't listen.
Things seem the same, my children, but
They aren't.

ICCO: Intellectual Construction Company

I wanted to change the world
But couldn't stand the smell in the streets.
Instead, I had perspicuous thoughts.
I spoke only when spoken to,
Parroted the eternal, moist banalities.
In these insincerities I felt I was a criminal.
When would they realize that I
Was not one of them, that I was unconvinced?
I had no image of my rise and did not fear my fall.
I lacked a motto and studied disenchantment.

Salesmen would come into the office
To sell the company concrete.
"What good is your concrete?" I wished to say.
"Who cares if there are more bridges,
Highways, jetports? What is the point of going places
When you aren't happy no matter where you are?
Why are you destroying the earth?"

The salesmen sucked on mouth-freshening mints
And squeezed my limp hand. I read Nietzche
At lunch over my hamburger and Coke.
The mordant mark of teleology was on me.
Employees phoned me with stories.
One's wife had run away, one's wife had come back,
One had wrecked his car, one had bought a car.
Whatever it was, they needed money.
I said I would tell the boss

When he got back from Milwaukee. I posted
Bail money three times and wondered how people
Got into such troubles. The secretaries downstairs
Kept smiling at me. Why was I carrying that book?
Did I mean to assault someone with it?

They shared insights about their friends' friends' friends.
No echo of gossip was too faint for them.
Each day I turned a page of a desk calendar
That advertised pre-stressed, reinforced, cement piers.
Outside, maple blossoms fell and were crushed against
The sidewalk and began to decay in the rain.
I wondered if it was possible to escape my unbuilding mind.

For My Brother Who Died before I Was Born

Pearly and opaque boy, it was you
To whom as a god
I furtively prayed before
I launched a marble
Or played a decisive card.

I made lists of the reasons why:
Certain teachers and times of year
And the failure of my team
To score runners from third—
Those were things to make you die.

I meant to ferret
My own mortality.
I mocked my mocking breath
And deftly smoked
Too many cigarettes.
At night I heard footsteps, high-pitched
Voices. Once, I saw a face in a candle flame.

Your absence was a game
That might at any move
Intrude upon my wanting life.
My hand fit in your old ball glove.
My dream was real:
Imagination is the proof of love.

From *Atoms, Soul Music and Other Poems* (1989)

The Single Urge

Peggy Everett, my first girlfriend, explains
That she is not so much leaving me as going
To someone else. I look at her as if
She were a mountain top in the next county.
Later, I try to educate the mirror in my room
But the mirror is not interested. It is only me
On a certain day, short in stature and short
Of knowledge, keen on the mechanics of desire.

I stay up late and try to imagine what it
Is like to be in her body. How can pleasure be
Confused? We had agreed, and I still agree
With the single urge that leans out windows, scribbles
Names in the margins of notebooks and is always
Ready to merge with what it lacks, what it believes.

Kitchen, 1952

I.

It was the kitchen of that
New house to which she moved
In 1952
That proved to my mother
The strength of her ascent.

The world was hers in a room
Possessed of oracular
Cleanliness, each surface ready
To stand the test of any
Dissolute spillage,
Each door and drawer and appliance
Instantly capable.

The plastic clock shaped
Like an apple might have smiled
Without educated irony
Upon this smiling housewife.
Modernity was a domestic dream.

II.

To my mother, the magazines'
Full-color layouts
Of efficient plenty must
Have embodied a timeless

114

Yet comfortable eloquence,
Poised at the peak
Of an affordable hope.

She looked about her,
Unbewildered, serene with
The wisdom of her female calling,
Buttressed by a phalanx of names—
GE, Frigidaire, Amana—
That bespoke the vigor of industry.
The white metallic silence answered.

III.

We children shrieked at spinach,
Sawed our way through roasts,
Clamored for the sugary
Vapors of packaged cake mix.
Dad came home late from work again.

Our little deaths are so
Predictable, yet remain
Strange to us. The counters
And pots were cleared and cleaned
In the wheel of ancient work.
Daily, love shone and disappeared.

Another family heals
And fractures now in that
Solicitous kitchen.

My mother's life stands out
With the overwrought truth
Of disappointment, the promise
Of managed bounty
That so gradually broke.

Deviled eggs and fried
Chicken and fruit punch
Sit on the table
One languid June day.
My mother laughs as if
To mock her own perfection,
As if to say, "But look at
Our hunger, it is incomplete."

Soul Music

The Baltimore evening I saw
Otis and Aretha I knew
Kings and queens still existed:
Poised but get-down, a danceable valor,
The uncharted cry and sigh
Strive and jive
From the shook up ground of
Plead-it-on-your-knees love.

The founded nation no longer
Was diagrammatic;
Unsevered feeling fit
Into any shade of skin.
Unchurched sound was the test
Of civil progress.

Outside that night
Plate glass fractured like
A sobbing final tone,
A plea that brought white overseers
To the city on a Sunday
While the condemned frolicked
At everyone's expense.

Whole blocks burned gladly,
The tinder of democratic
Promise redeemed in anger,
The grandeur of performance

Burlesqued by riot,
The insurrection of running free.

I too protested:
Hadn't I been good?
Hadn't I endorsed
Both sympathy and force?
Didn't I love the music
As much as I could?

On the televised streets
I watched people dance,
Souls on fire with a passion
That sang of days
No ticket could touch.

Social Security

Each month a check and my grandmother's born-
Again turmoil, tears ranging from
   Foreshortened sobs of relief,
   Her old age enthroned
On the far shores of comfort—a suburban
Home full of cookies, sliced bread and TV's—
To tense declamatory grief that ended
   In tranquilizers and two
   Incommunicado days in bed.
All things had been possible in America.
Now there was this rectangular mélange—a little
Money, an official number and some punched-out
Squares that only made sense to machines.

Chances were I'd have to listen to the story
Of Shana Rosenblatt who led a strike
Of seamstresses in 1913 and had her arms
Broken by company thugs. Shana
   Was dead but the government
   Wanted Grandma to live.
It did not cheer her up. For a dollar
   I was willing to hear her
   Go on about Eugene Debs.
Even at the age of ten I understood
That America could only choose between
What is and what is—none of this
What-might-be stuff. What was it like

To break the arms of a shrieking woman? The men
Must have needed money badly. Perhaps they had
   Sick children at home.
   America had been full
Of sick children once. Grandma's sister, Reva,
Had died in an epidemic. Now if
We had a cough or sore throat we went
To Doctor Katz. Who could imagine a child dying?
   I turned on the TV
   And we watched Maverick
Reluctantly shoot a cheating braggart. Grandma cheered
And told me I needed a Stetson hat. She would
Buy me one. Only Americans wore hats like that.

   "This money is people,"
   She'd say when she gave
Me a dollar. I made out that I understood.
After all, there was a man's face on it.
Did George Washington know that he
Was going to become money? It must
Have been a funny feeling if he did.
Once, I took the bill and tore it up
   To see if it would put
   Itself back together,
To see if it had a life of its own. My grand-
Mother told me I was a fool and looked
At the pieces on the carpeted floor and spat.

for Jo Josephson

Dropping Acid at Aunt Bea and Uncle Harry's 40th Wedding Anniversary Celebration

The little candles dotting the rosette-bedecked
Sheet cake sway so demurely that the happy
Huffing and puffing comes as cosmic surprise,
An operatic act of gods.
                        What a wind is this breath!
Their eccentric niece, the one who went out west
But flew back for the party, still can see the flames
But tells no one.
                The flames are Bea and Harry
Who stand slightly wavering in the draught
Of the years but lambent, pleased to have survived
When others as notable and kind have died.
Their fat wet kisses burn yet to her
It feels good to taste these reconciled lives.
Each plastic glass holds a rolling sea.
Each hors d'oeuvres plate is brown and greasy.
Bea's sister, Dora, is crying passionately, peering
From her folding seat into an abyss of joy.

Soon, it will be time for swaying
To the feisty flats of a sweaty accordionist
And toupeed Sinatra-smitten vocalist.
The niece taps her spoon on a coffee cup
Knowing that the room will dance in that spacey
Way that rooms dance. The building will kick in too

And the street won't want to be forgotten nor will
The automobiles that have been standing around
For hours patiently waiting—they love locomotion.

Bea and Harry take the first steps and it feels
Like the Dionysian apogee: feet stomping,
Arms entwined, bulging torsos heaving with rhythm.
Everyone is suffused with music's heady juice.
The niece forgets her extremes, her rises and falls.
The writhing floor is level, for once and for all.

Pigeons

Even naturalists are uninterested in the pigeons
Who loiter everywhere in the cities,
Birds who have sullied themselves
By learning to live with man.
They prosper amid degradation;
They are solicitous and indifferent, unanxious;
They feel they will live another day.
Their instincts are attuned
To the current extent of prodigal carelessness.

Kernels of whimsical saintliness
Fall from the hands of old men and women
Dipping into paper bags full
Of peanuts, bread crusts, fruit peels, seeds.
Like myths, pigeons eat everything.
Often they are parti-colored in invariably unattractive ways.
The old people fondle them with words,
Gurgles, gestures, litanies of off-key love.
The pigeons congregate like gangs,
Strut like overweight soldiers, shit and make
An officious mockery of flight.

Their tamed birdiness calls to our humanness.
They offer odd sounds, caricatures, the riches of self-absorption.

Listen to their vague digestion,
To their thoughts that are tiny as silica.
Adroit as settlers,

Neither romantics nor classicists,
The pigeons cover corporate plazas, benches, curbs, walkways,
Unconcerned with agony,
Grinding corn, investigating the wonders of gum.

Near Skowhegan

In the late October light
The town and mill and river glow
With good-for-nothing beauty.
All magnitude is here in
The light of emptiness and fullness,
The cup the sun drains every day.
Stand still and you can feel it:
The wind honing the shore,
The glare crazy on the glass panes,
A pointed chill in the air.
Exhilarating, how no one cares.

Once the water made the mill go
And people watched the river closely.
Once the town held a promise
Of free-born prosperity.
Now it's a place to work
For those who know work
As Eden's corporate curse.
When the shift lets out, everyone
Sniffs at this air, amazingly
Clear and clean and sweet.
Some hold the attitude for seconds,
Then open car doors carefully
As if entering a vault.

Starting the First Fire, Autumn

Once again we start to act hospitably.
Today we blacked the stove, swept up
The spiders from the wood box, split kindling.
Tonight's frost recalls debilities
More thorough than a chill or twinge.
We didn't perish like plants; we weren't houseflies:
The pungence of brevity was our false pride.

Now warmth suffices for philosophy.
The fire says it is the fire it was before,
That there is only one fire, the way
There is only a single earth or sky.
My hand in the light is faintly freckled but
Age doesn't figure in this basic mathematic.
Fire is not calculable like bodies.

We keep living the same life over and over...
Distinction blurs like embers turning cold.
We sit beside this familiar heat
On a night so deep it could never be rehearsed.

for Janet

From *When* (1997)

Listening to a Baseball Game

The smothering heat of a July night
Squats in a second-floor bedroom
And doesn't move despite the desk fan's
Peaceful whir and simulate breeze.
A boy lies on the sheets and reads
A *Life* magazine which holds
The proper shadow of attention
While he listens to the ballgame
Being played in Kansas City.
He sees it happen and imagines it—
The same thing really. A car swings

Down Maple Street, a hinge complains.
Moths move toward decipherable light
But are baffled by screens. The boy's done
Reading and lies there beside the lamp,
His hands folded beneath his head.
He knows that comfort is rarely pure.
He listens and lets his feelings glide
With each intent description.
He follows a probable dream
As the night sways with outcomes
In houses and rooms and far away.

for Charles Baxter

Poems

In July, under the sign of Cancer when Vega climaxes,
it's small firearms time. A modest piece carries a strong message.
At several thousand feet, doors splinter like kindling.
Up close, to a person, it's a splatter.
People are rivers. They're dammed up rivers.

The sound's so short, it's like a comma, not even
an exclamation mark. It's a high, groaning pop.

Uncle Ed shows me his complete arsenal—at least fifteen
weapons of various calibers. "An armed citizenry is the best
defense against tyranny." He says that to me. He got
laid off two years short of retirement. He security guards
for two bucks over minimum wage. "It's not a cop, but it's
not not a cop," he says over Aunt Minna's thick coffee.

No one much recognizes a name in a newspaper, a shooting name—
no one's looking at a paper for that knowledge—
unless maybe you're a student teacher for a semester in
the city and you know it's that kid, Rinaldo. He liked
to do long division. One day he told you not to interrupt
him with your foolishness. He was learning something. He was
a couple of months over eleven.

You're up late reading Rilke. The poems drift like swans
on a rippling pond. Later, you're in the car on the way to the Cape.
The darkness breeds reverie;
The luminescence of *once upon* beckons.

130

You catch yourself awaiting a siren, the trumpet
of someone's doom. *"...hinter tausend Stäben keine Welt"*:
you turn off the a/c, yawn disconsolately.

Poetry is the logic beyond reason. That's what keeps you reading
all these twitchy nights. Inside the tread of days and years
there's a labyrinth. On its walls are candles of words. They
bruise the illimitable shadows. You pull the car off the road,
get out, feel the soft salt of the breeze. You shiver. Back
in the city another kid is eating the trigger.

In the lockup someone's shouting "motherfucker" fairly loudly
but no one's interested. In your room it's deep in the middle
of the night and you're sleeping. You're dreaming. You see so
many faces each day in the subway, on the streets. Every moment
is expressive and it flows into you like some grand river out
west. Your soul's a canyon. And their souls too.

American Poem of the Senior Citizenry

I. Arizona

The lungers stick together, as do
The arthritic, the lame and those
Who are mysteriously whole.
Everyone protests his or her vigor
While comparing coughs and cures,
Telephone calls from successful children.
Immaculate cells litter the landscape
Where lizards breed and gods came forth
From the weatherless sky.
Immaculate lawns invoke the peace
Of pebbles, light posts, asphalt.
Even the ambulances are quiet.

If life repeats the same anecdote,
One must be thankful for blessed tedium.
Something else could happen, something
Headshaking, dizzy, abrupt.

Everyone celebrates birthdays
With the passion of partying children:
Another hot dog, feigned distress
And that old singsong the wavering voices
Never want to let go.

II. Florida

Steinberg,
        The most garish philosophies prosper
In this place. Every other widow is
A cardsharping, Zionist, diet-mystic.
The ones-in-between follow the stock
Market the way we rooted for
The Polo Grounds Giants.
Young, naked bodies are everywhere.
Tribes of them bow down before
The sun like New-Age Mayans.
The corned beef, though, is good
And there is condoed culture:
Mozart in Miami, chess games
That placate eternity,
Lending libraries as eager to dispense
Murder mysteries as history.
This is no place to die,
Which is why we are here.
Our resentments against our old lives
Dwindle mercifully. I no longer
Wake up wishing to choke that
Swindling two-timer Sternblatt.
This is what America calls "contemplative,"
Where you find the courage perhaps
To realize you never grasped what it was
You so diligently and lengthily did.
Red sails in the sunset, Steinberg,
And dividend checks in the mail.

III. Farm

Not many people know as much about
Silence as a farmwife does.
She has the quiet keys.
She could be a cat.
Solitary labor, Ralph used to call it.
He worked and worked, I worked and worked.
The children grew like trees.
How many times I looked out that kitchen
Window at games of ball, rain, a balky heifer.
It was gone even as I looked
And I understood that.
People fear the land.
They gather in cities and they talk,
Always talking like on the damn TV.
This country doesn't know enough to shut up.
You can be too strong, of course, too silent,
But that's the earth's element.
It's empty here and it was
And I hope it always will be.

IV. The Home

Dosage charts phantasms of pain
The doctor from some foreign country
The teenage girls who remove the bedpans

One morning sure begins to look like another

The phenomenal cheerfulness
As relentless as the body

No summary will do

Playing hearts and bingo
Cheating scrupulously

The stages between life and death

As when a tree dies or a soul must
Make a perilous journey
Traveling through jello catheters pills
Invisible to the workaday eye

Buttoning buttons very carefully

Weeping old-fashioned rich weeping
Over abandonments illusions
The mirth of such friendly strangers

Rudinsky's, 1953

In the back of my grandfather's delicatessen
The waiters talked about the bad things.
Dropping dishes, that was more than bad,
It was a curse, a shame on the profession.
That's what they called it, a profession.
Nowadays that means sitting through college
And being rewarded for your persistence
But there was a lot to it—you had to be swift
And deft, you had to be strong, you had to be patient,
You had to be calm. Lots of qualities.

Like monkeys, diners had busy hands.
They weren't there only to eat. The families
Maybe but the couples had other thoughts.
But the bad things—slipping was a bad thing,
Not adding up a check correctly, setting
The wrong dish down, forgetting to pour the water.
The waiters watched for each other and looked out for each other.
They were mothers and brothers to each other.

Have you ever been on your legs for ten hours straight?
Do it for thirty years and we'll talk about it.

The waiters knew everything there was to know
About the human disgrace (as they called it).
To keep their wits alert they bet on the size
Of a tip before a party sat down. They bet
On how many drinks, which desserts, sugar in

The coffee, trips to the can.
Clothes, eyes, manners, speech—
Each social tic was a fact or hint.
Every conceivable peril had happened:
Fainting spells, sulphurous farts, screaming fits,
Broken glass, drunks, check skippers.
A reputable joint with a cop out front but people
Were people no matter how tasty the brisket was:
Women stuffed pickles in their pocketbooks,
Men grabbed handfuls of toothpicks.
The worst thing was a lady making eyes at you.
Only misery could come of that. One night
A fellow threw a plate of blintzes at a waiter,
"Bothering my girl, you lousy Jew."
The waiters shook their heads and made disgusted faces.

You could know everything, that was the funny part,
But it didn't help. As in a dream you saw
It before it was going to happen but still it happened—
Like the Nazis or rain or when you go to get
The last piece of cheesecake and it's not there.

It's a Party (1959)

The rhododendron is happy. Its aloof yet sexual
   Blossoms glimmer in the cool April moonlight.
The pebbles in the driveway croon very softly.
The ceramic Negro jockey, which toward the end of the next
   decade the children who are now asleep in
   their Snuggy-Pooh pajamas will unceremoniously
   smash as a honky racist artifact, extends an arm
   of welcome.
People drink, eat and talk elaborately:
   It's the death of Charlie Parker
   A grandma who swims eighty laps at the Y
   Crab cake recipes
   Zoning bribes
   Sartre's existential pride.
If everyone is aware of everyone else,
   everyone is unconcerned too.
The halftones of sex
   craft a jauntily steamy mood
   of nods and titters, long and longer looks.
It's
Eric Dolphy
Trane
Charles Mingus
The brass panoply of subtle freedom
The bottom dog and top drawer.
It's
Life in the big adrenaline city
Life in shack-roof deputy-sheriff Mississippi

Life in a Nash Rambler looking out
    windows at oblivious trees.
It's
Miles of Miles
Miles Smiles
Miles' Unpredictable Wiles.

Winks and shrugs as soft as rayon.
People muse and kiss.
Someone in tight black pants is lying on his back
    contemplating the ceiling moldings.
Someone is ambling through a photo album—
    a heaven of lost moments.
Someone is downing abandoned drinks:
    bourbon, Scotch, sloe gin.
There's nothing like being drunk and skimming a page
    of Proust, as if you too were an epic of ephemera.
There's nothing like touching someone's skin
    you've wanted to touch for hours.
There's nothing like pronouncing an enlightened opinion,
    then mocking yourself seconds later
    for being so fucky-ducky holy.

Someone hoots like a startled owl.
Someone flings peanuts into his mitt of a mouth.
Someone yawns fiercely
    while the jazz the lofty gritty searching
    elegantly churning jazz
    the sympathetic overheard genius plays on.

Swayed

A boy, I marked a circle around a tree,
A hobbling line on a tethered winter's day.
I meant to cordon infinity;
I meant to guard what I could not say

Yet felt obscurely. A conjuring clattering stick
In my right hand I struck at horizons
And heights. I would perform a human trick,
One that answered the wan dying sun

In the rose-hazed west. That first thrilling chill
Of death in the late afternoon, the tiny power
That tastes extinction like snow in the still
Air and rejoices that the ultimate hour

Is distant, unknown. I was blood-magic
And swayed beneath the fir tree like a cantor,
Intoning nubs of sounds, gesturing with quick
Unpracticed jerks. Absurd no doubt or

Something simpler. I see the boy alert
In near darkness, head back to absorb the sky—
A veil laid over an ancient earth,
The truest irrelevant guide.

Sonnet

When the troops don't find the trade union
Leader at home (some intelligence misconstrued),
They swear and look for someone else to ruin:
A shrieking girl of twelve will have to do.
They stuff her mouth with gloves; they tear her sex
Like cellophane; they force her anus, then beat
Her skull with the butt of a rifle until flecks
Of bone obtrude. Now, they have not been cheated.

They light machine-rolled cigarettes and go.
When next evening, the priest arrives, he smells
The smoke of candles. His breath stalls but after slow
Steep seconds it returns, the knell
Of life. *If then he fell, he might not rise.*
He speaks—so that what is human might die.

Children's Ward

Accident Face tells Breathless to let go,
It's not her toy, it's his. She drops the plastic gun
And stings him with her X-ray eyes.
He might be a bug or painting. "Oh, Monster Boy,"
She hisses, "Halloween is history.
You don't need a mask." Her skull tilts back.
Her laugh is amusement and nonchalant fright.

Two baldies are wheeled in from chemo.
Empty Heart has messed himself and is whining.
"But he's always whining," the Princess of Pain
Explains to her rag doll. "He likes to whine."
Winter light scouts the dirty windows.
Mourning doves moan. There's a sky.

The TV gambols but the beds are brisk and
Neat as lined paper or utopian cities.
If you make enough motions you might go home.
You lecture your tumors and talk to your bones.
It's work to stare at the wincing lights—
A mirror might leap at you, a nurse.
It's work to eat, to search out your voice,
To smile at the smiles, to sleep when it's night.

Everyone gets tired so fast. "Last century," the Princess
Says to Short Legs, "we'd all be dead.
We'd all be sleeping the everlasting sleep.

We'd never know what it's like to be even as old
As ten is. We'd be mummies, creeps..."

Practice makes tenacity perfect; hope keens more than
It sighs. Somewhere, children are not thinking.
"But we," the Princess says, "must live in this story."

On the Bus to Houston

Smashing sticks of gum till her jaw smarts,
Looking for something out there to look at,

Some scenery while the guy beside her
Keeps stretching his mouth but says nothing.

He gives off a crazy-type vibe: he could
Lose it any minute and not know it.

He's going to touch her—she knows it.
She's sat on more than one daddy's knee

And doesn't want the littlest touch of those hands.
The book in her lap stays shut—a mystery,

People talk to each other, kill each other.
It makes a kind of heartless sense.

She's wearing black though no one in her life has died.
It's her traveling dress; it keeps people quiet.

In a pale taunting way she's pretty:
As if that mattered, as if there were

An honest man to whom she could say
That her beauty has been a joke.

The guy's going to fall asleep.
He looks sort of dog-like sweet.

He isn't though. She's too educated
About the wrong things. Somewhere in books,

Her twin is alive. She's not better
Or worse. What she is, is clear,

As if someone cleaned a body, cleaned
It till it glowed like nobody's dream.

Cow Symphony

Ovals of crushed September stubble
Where the weight has rested quilt the field.
The ambling towards the block of salt,

The algae-mouthed pond, tree shade
Or blade, stalk, leaf, kernel
Or what seems like movement for the sake

Of movement, purity of motive uncommonly
Encountered. Whimsical tonnage
Pissing and shitting unfugitively.

Beautiful globular eyes, demure tails,
Rough colors—browns Cezanne loved—
Always applied variously to

Each canvas of hoofed being.
Stomachs that cannot be seen.
Calves frolic, kindled, surging

With breath, blood, breeze, bodyness,
Bucking gravity, greeting ground.
Molten bellows, squeals, pacific grunts,

Cloppings, settling sighs and fearful
Stubborn bovine bleats when the truck
Comes to collar what seemed so hugely free.

for Janet

Vegas: the Urge

Driving into Las Vegas at dusk
We stop spewing our desert-bred
   denunciations
And gawk, the apes of amazed lust.

It's one hot-pink, neon fire
After another as the autos pulse forward,
   platelets
On the stream of talking desire.

There's no finale to shrewdly strike
And we love that. It's like money
   moving
From hand to shaky hand; it's like

Flesh fine as a showgirl wearing
A lace collar and nothing else or
   flaccid
As the old women fumbling in their

Suitcase-sized pocketbooks. It's
The end that doesn't end: day and
   night
Dancing like Dantean lovers, wits

Fried in a paradise where wealth
Is gospel-shouting, testifying to
 the urge
That's a sex unto its warm self.

Fans

When Janis Joplin died,
       Some people smiled, buoyant in their malice,
            then noted
To one another over
            unflappable newsprint
       That she had it coming,
a bad woman, dope user
   And that finger-pointing,
            pin-the-tail-on-the-evils-of-excess thing.

       I went out back of the house and cried
   Till I was spent from crying.
            I lay on the October ground
But felt no peace
   and felt I never would gain peace
       on this planet of pursy fatalists.

       My friend Raymond insisted
   That white people shouldn't mix with the blues,
       they couldn't handle it.

Two weeks before, Hendrix had died.
   Raymond shrieked on the phone to me,
All our slang seemed
            like a child's uneasy bravery.

            I played their records
   And felt again how they turned terror into

                    a good time:
He was bent-note wry; she was grievously kind.
        Both throbbed
                with blooded, give-it-up, orgasm-scream
                    voodoo—
Throwing some strobe
                in the cautious tomb, goosing the gods of ordinariness,
Outraging a day shift doom.

  If it was bad,
        it was bad
            the way rain ran down
A hotel's grimy sealed windows,
        a little gray drama
                when the singing and sex were over
                    and you awoke imperfectly
        To a first
Twitching cigarette, your manager's demands
                    and the echo
Of those imploring fans.

  Out in the cheering dark we remain,
            chanting joy's refrains.
    In the dire quick moments
        nothing has changed.

Bob Ward (1955)

Two nights a week Bob Ward the insurance man
Whose office stood beside the hardware store
Got in his car and drove to other rooms
In other towns to meet another man.
They loved—and held a joy that terrified
The sickly thrall of day. The words that seemed
To probe his every moment fell away.
The hell of every shame and fear, each nod
And smile, the famous business handshake
Unplumed in the cock's hard grace. He prayed
For himself later in the clock-bound dark.
He prayed for the bachelor soul that seemed
Not pith but fog. He wept a few glad tears
And watched the sun sneak up: the slightest pink
Flame simmered on the horizon. He chose a tie
To match his suit, then headed to the cafe—
"Mornin', Bob"—where he took his determined place.

Delmore Schwartz

Within one human being the fifty-seven
Varieties of bedevilment
Coexisted incautiously, eager to salt,
Infect and leaven poem, story, essay or letter
With an American-buckshot, Yiddish-comic,
Late-Elizabethan, college-cafeteria rhetoric.
He was present the way children hold their hands up
To indicate that yes they are there,
Ready, in this case, to dun the muse,
Flatter the damnable world, be damned one's self
In operatic yet colloquial fashion:
One day Hal, the next Antony—
All the while trying to make stretched ends meet,
All the while dabbling in coterie civilities,
All the while diving into seductive buoyancies.
He could hear Eliot discreetly brooding
Across the ocean; he could smell the competition—
A bucolic waft up through a subway grate
And on into the airplane-ridden empyrean.

A poet is an unsuitable joke able
To mimic any legend of the past thousand years.
A poet's heart is a well that has
No Apollonian bottom—and a modern heart
At that, looking backwards when no one is noticing,
Promulgating its inventive energy,
Searching out the cabals of grown-up boys' clubs,
Lubricating the influence

Of a horse-playing uncle who knows a cop who knows
A judge who can get you into the *Anglican-*
Cum-Jewish Pan-fried New Critical Review.

Souls clap hands in the Hollywood night.
Get-rich schemes sprout like mushrooms in Poland.
Let's call up Shakespeare. What would he say?
The receiver hums in your wieldy hands.
Someone is going to reply to
The vaudevillian vicar's summary
Of the last days of eternity: cakes and despair
In the cozy purlieus of East Coca-Cola.
Someone is going to reply.
In the meantime, poet, wait.

My Wife Asks Me Why I Keep Photographs
in a Drawer

Beneath tee shirts and underwear
A few almost-sepia photographs
Of my mother and father—before they knew me.

My mother stands in front of the school
Where she first taught fourth grade.
She's young and lovely and smiling
In a summer dress. Her shoulders are bare,
Her eyes alight with candid feeling.
The year before she worked
In a department store where she read Tolstoy
During her breaks. One day she came back
To her counter red-eyed; her supervisor inquired
About her. "Anna died," my mother blurted.

My father sits at a table. He holds some cards
And smiles. The other guys at the table
Are soldiers too and they smile. They're going
To live through the war. It's aces and swell
Broads and highballs and homeruns for them.

I should set up a shrine for these
Bouquets of time, something more visible.
They lie there quietly as I stutter through
My slice of time—from semi-hippiedom
To that bill-paying, fitful sleep
That signals a flagging of mortal belief.

I never take them out. I know them too well.
It's dark in the drawer and common and hidden.
Photos show that people can smile
At the dull eye of oblivion. Albums and walls
Insist too much. What's part of each fumbling
Morning is nearer to the fleeting mark.

Hettie Smith

When Hettie Smith our maid would quit, she'd tell
My mother that as an employer she was
"Unfeeling, unclean and unholy." My mother
Would start to blubber and protest her love.
If I was present, I wondered who in this sweaty
World was holy. A few days later
Hettie would return quietly; dust drowsed again.

Hettie told me that white people thought they
Knew so much about colored people but they didn't.
In fact, white folks were simple as infants.
"You imagine a grown man in a diaper—that's
A white man. Colored folks are here to sanctify
The world. It says so in the Bible," Hettie said.
I'd read Bertrand Russell and told her the Bible
Was a lie. She turned from her mopping to slap me
As deftly as a cat swats a mouse. "The Lord have mercy
On you," she intoned prayerfully. "The Lord have mercy."

One sweltering day she had a stroke on the number
Four streetcar. She died right there.
At her funeral her son Lawrence denounced
Us as exploiters and devils. It was the 60s.
I bit my lip and looked around warily
As if I had blinders on or dark glasses.
Emmeline, Hettie's oldest daughter, rose up
And said that there was no place for hate on this day,
That hate dried up the rivers of our hearts.

Years later Lawrence sent us a brief letter.
We weren't evil, he wrote, just well-meaning.

I think of the judgments we make
About ironing shirts and wiping tables
And cooking pot roast and taking an aspirin,
How we grind each day on the lathe of experience
And marvel at the unappeased friction,
And I think of Hettie's slap, her flower-print dresses,
The petite mole on her right cheek and her faith
That was as approachable as it was strong.

1978

A couple of years after the bicentennial
Once the fire of self-congratulation had simmered down
To the normal frenzy of electro-Jeffersonian desire
We headed west in one of my younger brother's three Chevs—
Uninsured and fast. Officially (a send-off party) and unofficially
(No tee-shirts) The Nuclear Bullet Tour, in which
We left the comfortably filthy streets, airshafts
And ethnic snacks of Brooklyn behind,
The human grid of orderly transience, to sniff out
Missile silos, the long knife in America's back pocket,
To go underground as Dante did once upon a time
Even though it was in a poem.
Not being in a poem, we figured we could go him
One better, take a gander at the control panels of Dis,
A brightly-lit, well-ventilated if claustrophobic crèche—
Part-Hollywood, part mannish hypno-tech.

Meanwhile, canyons, rivers and mountains, majesty
That makes words evaporate, glimpses of aeons
In the geology that dwarfs our monist Sundays.
We drank a good-sized farm pond worth of coffee,
Kept earnest journals that make me want to cry
Now when I read them: the sunrises outside Nowhere,
Glinting breezes (I wanted to write "zephyrs"),
The half-inch of dew, we camerados lying there
In sleeping bags, warm and waiting for the sky.

Somewhere beyond Omaha a cop pulled us over
For a dead taillight. No ticket or hassle,
Your where-you-boys-from kind of cop.
The closest we got to the beast was a checkpoint
In North Dakota. We said we were taxpayers
And the guard smiled about three teeth's worth of a smile.
"Who are you assholes kidding?" he said.
Hard to argue with him.
I guess we thought the earth would open up somehow.
We chanted over the 327, "Nuke Spook, Nuke Spook."

"Those bombs help people, they never gonna be used,"
An old-timer told us one morning in a cafe in Montana.
"You boys got yourselves worked up about nothin'.
Only a fool would fuck this place up." He gestured with
The stump of an arm he retained from WWII.
We spent a few days at his ranch
Moseying around on horses so intelligent and mild
Even we could ride them.
                    On the way home
We stopped at a bar on the endless outskirts
Of Chicago whose cinder block façade
Possessed the warm allure of a bomb shelter
And where we bought a round of mixed drinks
For the four people in there at two o'clock on a gray
Afternoon. "To hell," we proposed. No one demurred.

For Pleasure (Bob Corin's Pickup)

I'm driving in my pickup, which is a Ford
Because Ford built America and I respect that
Though the Pilgrims were go-getters too coming over
Here in those little wooden boats they had to be crazy
Or believers like the Four Square Gospel people or both
And Karen's with me right up snug against me.
I hate it when you look in a truck and there's air
Between a man and a woman, she's sitting at one end
Thinking about a refrigerator and he's at the other
End thinking about bird hunting and that's
All their lives are is their damn thoughts.
I'm trying to get a song on the radio but I'm
Getting the news which is about some Russians and
The White House, though it's their White House not ours.
They're fighting about something.
Karen wants a Softserve at the Dairy Delite
Which is swell because I like to see her tongue
Go dabbling in that sweet stuff. You can't beat
A tongue for pleasure. It must have been hell
When they used to cut people's tongues out.
I'd rather go blind. Now it's the Stock Market,
Which I could give a shit about.
The only person I knew who cared about that
Was Billy Thompson the lawyer's son who was
The only boy in the French Club in high school
And it wasn't on account of the girls.
He liked French. Which is sort of sad to my mind.
Anyhow, I put my money into my truck. It's got

161

Chrome-plated tailpipes and a set of mud flaps
With Yosemite Sam on them saying, "Back Off!"
I was born to customize.

I start to mash the gas pedal down because I'd like
To drive right out of this poem but I can't of course.
I'm like one of those clowns that Shakespeare
Liked to make fun of, though clown
Doesn't mean make-up and a red nose like at
The Shrine circus. It means a rustic, someone
Who prefers living to talking about living.
Writers fear life so they make art. Which
Is cozy and I can't blame them. Karen's burning
A hole in my thigh. She's rubbing her thigh against
Mine kind of distracted-like and I'd just as soon
Stay with her in this rapid box until next week.
I'm not credible, I'm not predictable, I'm not malleable.
I wish I could eat every word in Karen's spacious mouth.

The Entertainer

I'm fifty-six years of age, which means
My shirt has a hard time covering my gut
And under my chin and jaw the skin's starting
To hang like a wet washcloth and I'm singing
About love.
There was a time when that word
Had something to say to my life but it's
Been awhile, it's been awhile.

Still, there's a body blow called divorce out there
And the crowd—from around thirty-five to the early
Fifties—likes the oldies, like the safety
And slow ecstasy of the past.
As do I. The songs stay young although
The people don't and I like it when I look
Out over the dance floor, which could be in a bar
Or a gym or an armory or some godforsaken hall

Built in the last century for farmers or preachers
And I see the couples close to each other, the women
Resting themselves against the men and the men
Standing tall but trying to relax and the sex urge
Going back and forth between them like an electric charge.
I like that because it's formal but it's human.
I like that because people don't get to dance much,
They're busy being beauticians and teachers and contractors.

It's Sock Hop Night or Golden Memories
And I'm down on my creaky knees pleading
That when I lost my baby I almost lost my mind
And the sax player, who's half my age and tokes up
Before each show although I tell him I don't want him
Wrecked or sit-on-his-ass mellow, is moaning
Like the god of fornication and I know we're telling
The truth, the misplaced but never lost truth.

A Quiet Life

What a person desires in life
   is a properly boiled egg.
This isn't as easy as it seems.
There must be gas and a stove,
   the gas requires pipelines, mastodon drills,
   banks that dispense the lozenge of capital.
There must be a pot, the product of mines
   and furnaces and factories,
   of dim early mornings and night-owl shifts,
   of women in kerchiefs and men with
   sweat-soaked hair.
Then water, the stuff of clouds and skies
   and God knows what causes it to happen.
There seems always too much or too little
   of it and more pipelines, meters, pumping
   stations, towers, tanks.
And salt—a miracle of the first order,
   the ace in any argument for God.
   Only God could have imagined from
   nothingness the pang of salt.
Political peace too. It should be quiet
   when one eats an egg. No political hoodlums
   knocking down doors, no lieutenants who are
   ticked off at their scheming girlfriends and
   take it out on you, no dictators
   posing as tribunes.
It should be quiet, so quiet you can hear
   the chicken, a creature usually mocked as a type

of fool, a cluck chained to the chore of her body.
Listen, she is there, pecking at a bit of grain
    that came from nowhere.

From *Mulroney.and Others* (2000)

Mulroney

Where the hell do these people come from?
Mulroney asked me.
We were crumpling up a Sunday *New York Times*
That had found its way into the pile of papers
We used as packing filler for glass jars of honey.
We were wadding up the wedding notices—
Young lawyers in love with account executives.
Their fathers were surgeons and vice-presidents;
Their mothers were psychologists and counselors.

We were working as prep cooks at a ski resort
And packing boxes at a place down in the valley
To make a couple extra bucks.
Mulroney didn't know anything except
Eat, fuck, sleep, ski. A regular physical guy,
He barely knew what Vietnam was
And it was 1975.
He could have lived any time or place,
And for all ostensible purposes he was.
He'd wake in the morning in the cold cabin
We shared and he'd curse
And try to coax whatever woman he was sleeping
With to start the fire in the wood stove.
I could hear him cooing in his gravelly
Flattened brogue. Occasionally
The woman would rise, most mornings
She would tell him what to do with himself.
Defeats and victories and

Sunlight licking the frosted windows
And Mulroney full of the dumb sap of time
And scratching his balls.

Where the hell do these people come from?
He asked me.
Mulroney, you dim honky ass, I said.
They are groomed to run the show
And he looked down at the crumpled vivacity
Of the young brides in newsprint
And he broke into an almost lovely smile
And he said in a voice that could have
Passed for thoughtful, How sad.

The Tape

Around eleven-thirty Al's fallen asleep
And you zap the TV with the remote
Because late night has never been your thing.
Those smiles like new clothes,
Those voices like prom kings and queens
As if every night were the big date.
You have to wonder about people
So eager to talk about themselves.
Probably nothing much has happened to them,
They were too busy smiling.

You put on the videotape of Claudia
Cooking in her eighth grade Home Ec class,
And she's wearing a blue corduroy jumper
That could have been hemmed better,
And she's got on those dingy braces that
Doc Eastley claimed would do the trick
But it doesn't matter much what Doc thought
Because Claudia was in the car that
Sheila Hersheimer who was all of sixteen
Was driving that strayed across the center
Line (as they said in the newspaper) into
The path of a one-ton GMC truck.

What do you do this for?
Aren't your nights harrowed enough already?
Aren't your eyes sick with seeing
The same once-upon-a-person over and over?

Isn't your soul so dismal that rising
In the weak morning is more a dream than a life?
Of course you know the answer—
She's alive on that tape and that's what
You want to feel, her being alive.
It's not complicated and it's not as wrong-
Headed as the therapist insists it is
Because you know she's dead and you can
Feel her spirit leaving yours little by little
Each day, a real slow seepage,
Like summer turning into autumn.
The tape seems to stop that,
The tape is a slap in your stupid face.

Al's snoring. His sinuses
Are getting worse. Probably you should move south.

You stop the tape, stare at the blue screen
For a while, hear your own strangely rapid breathing.
We're born ignorant and we build on that,
You think. The tape will break one of these days.
God will fall from the sky one of these days,
Yet some part of you is happy—
As if you had met someone you hadn't seen
In a long time and had found some true feeling
That had been lost. Some part of you is happy to feel
The tingle of a child's life.

You turn on the TV and some guy
With every hair neatly in place, as if it were
A dried grass arrangement, is telling a story

About an ex-wife. Or maybe it's an ex-life.
You used to be a believer too in your way.
And when you close your eyes you see a girl
Holding up a wooden spoon and twirling it
Like a baton.

Zbigniew Herbert's Mr. Cogito Meets Emily Dickinson: A Literary Romance

The minuet of extroversion is not exquisite.
Although Mr. Cogito has taken lessons from
A dancing master prosperous enough to maintain
A studio in a respectable neighborhood,
He distrusts the patterned movements of balls.
Formal pleasure is not genuine pleasure, he feels.
Meanwhile, the vagaries of the gentry are encyclopedic.
The pursuit of delight is an ordeal.
Mr. Cogito's shoes pinch.

He prefers to dance with a ghost.
She is curiously halting, angular,
Her witticisms have a distinctly metaphysical cast.
Her tokens of favor include a clump
Of cat hair, an itchy mitten, a murmur.
Her smile is beautifully homely.

Mr. Cogito is the object of derision and compassion.
A countess invites him to lunch.
Her gloved hands inveigle his.
A large landowner with a hirsute voice invites
   him to shoot grouse.

Mr. Cogito hears the rustle of fearless skirts
A moth in winter
A candle breathing.

He begins to write verses on scraps of paper
Broken epigrams
Spendthrift metaphors.

He refuses the last dance
As a young woman whirls through the mazurka
With a gallant young captain.

Mr. Cogito peers out a window
Into the night.
Soon he will be home in his
Little room, a book in his hands,
Pursuing heaven and earth.

Goethe in Kentucky (1932)

Imagine (my mother said) two German Jews
Plunked down in Kentucky in the 1930s:
Mules and Model T's and monosyllables
Like banjo twangs and that brown tobacco
Dribble that was so casually barbarous.

Imagine Herman and Clara and their two suitcases:
No silver candlesticks to celebrate Shabbos,
No leather bound books, no Goethe
That all-purpose sage-artist who equably
Plumbed the demonic channels of human casuistry
Yet sang like a cheerful Greek bird,
Who loved Italy and his bit of Germany.

Imagine Goethe in Kentucky and you can see
Some of what it must have been like for
Herman and Clara, how they looked around
Timidly and boldly, knowingly and unknowingly,
Since this was the same earth
But transposed into an improbable key.

Imagine them learning to go about
Their American business beneath
A soft spring sky lacy with clouds
And a sky dark as a hellfire preacher's Bible
And a sky blank with the torpor of summer.

Imagine them sitting at a kitchen table and puzzling out
The racial laws that applied to Negroes but
As the infamous Christ-killers might pertain to them—
The reach of loathing being at once particular
And not particular. Imagine the dance of deference,
Faces opaque as window shades, fears barbing
The simplest words, the baffling, Mandarin-Southern,
"Yes, ma'am" etiquette and the chilling, occasional howl
Of blood that bayed for a day or two before
Swooning like a dream into the sun of morning.

Imagine Goethe there at some crossroads in Kentucky
Looking at a tree or church or car
And shaking his beautiful, radiant head that loved
This world so deeply and he being thankful for his life
In this land that was so careless it could swallow like
A scrap of toast the rankest insanity.

Briefly

To stand and drop
Or toss or let fall any little available
   object
Into water.

To throw slush into an April stream
And gape at the soft second when semblance
   dissolves
Or spit into a puddle
Or skip a pebble on a pond
Or let a stone plummet
Or allow a bit of fluff to drift in the wind
   and
Eventually, out of the eye's reach but not the mind's,
   kiss the river below
Or scuff a bit of bark or moss or duff
   into
The thin ditch beside the road
Is to be seized by the plight of vertiginous
   wonder.

The hand that lets go
Seems godlike
             and the pang of that moment
When some minute presence
                    is borne away for good
Is dizzying
As the dry beech leaf rides

                    and bobs and darts
Or the snow turns gray
                        in the water and is gone
And the awful assumption of death
And the illusion of anything
                            being fixed in time
Are tangible
            and briefly imaginable.

In the Grocery

It's been around ten years since I'd seen
Tammy LaChapelle but I knew it was she
Standing in front of the dry cereals, not that
She was anyone special as a student—
"Special" means "special" which means one
Or two a year—but she read the books I told
Her to read and she wrote the papers.
She liked the Emily Dickinson poems we do
Every year but high school becomes history fast
And when I look in her face it's plain
That it hasn't been an easy decade:
There's a hardness in her eyes and around her lips
As if you couldn't buy a deep smile from her
And I know that story too well—when she
Was eighteen her boyfriend was twenty-five and she
Was riding around in a man's truck and she was balling
A man—not some schoolboy—every night that
She could sneak out of her house and she was a woman—
Adored, irresistible and available.

That must have gone to hell the way it usually does—
Him getting edgy and her getting bored and there'd be
Another and another, but she's always on her own, she's
Always alone even when a guy's right inside her
And she doesn't know what's going on because it's her
Raw body that turns them on like lights
And somehow she's more than that body.

180

It's not that I'm shrewd; it's that I've known
Twenty Tammies. I want to say that sex is a gauntlet
More than a blessing but instead I notice the little girl
Behind Tammy, blonde and wary, as Tammy says,
"Hi, Mr. Wormser." We stand there flat-footed for a few
Moments trading harmless inquiries,
But there's a tremor of pride in her voice—
It's her life and she's not crying to anyone.

We both turn to the boxes of flakes and oats
And we both look hard at them so as not to look
At each other and there are tigers and elves
And smiling children on the box fronts and we each
Pick up a box deftly and carefully as if we were big
And we were making a grown-up choice.

The Haircut

Dwayne Richardson had been growing
This Beatle hairdo that looked pretty
Dorky on him because his hair wasn't lank
And fine but more like a wavy wire brush.
One day grew into another until the principal
Invited Dwayne in for a chat (as he liked to put it)
And said he was going to suspend Dwayne
If Dwayne didn't get rid of that silly long hair.
It was an issue of honor and Dwayne replied,
"No sir," in a voice of deferential defiance.

During his week off, Dwayne hiked down to the recruiter's
Office in Portland and joined the Army.
He was in 'Nam in what seemed like no time
And no one thought much about him and then he was dead.
It was sketchy as to how it happened but he wasn't coming
Back alive and the principal said on the loudspeaker
One day that we'd lost a hero. By that time
The Beatles were starting to get pretty weird,
As were a lot of other people, and later Dwayne's sister
Patty said that another grunt in the platoon told her how he
And Dwayne used to smoke a bone some nights for their nerves
And talk about high school and music.

The first thing the Army had done was cut his hair.
"Irony is the oxygen of modern times," Mr. Hamilton,
The smartest of the four history teachers, used to say.
Maybe Dwayne didn't have him or if he did he was looking

182

Out the window at the sunshine when the teacher said it
Or he was humming "A Hard Day's Night" in his head or
He heard it quite distinctly and wrote it down in his notes
And paused and thought.

Melancholy Baby

(In memoriam, W. M.)

You sit at the end of the bar
Beneath the basketball game on the TV.
The people look at you partially,
Which suits your permanently pressed mood.
Though it's a different bar tonight
You order the usual. Contemplating too long
Tends to promote a triple shot of trouble.
Something exciting has happened in the game;
There's a briefly fervent look in people's eyes.
You peer into your drink. It's no Sargasso Sea
And you're no diver. There's something akin to joy
In being so world-weary.

You walk into the funeral home
And announce yourself as a business
Associate because we all are business
Associates in America even if
We high-mindedly try to ignore it or join
A transcendent cult or just blisslessly screw up
On what seems like our own.
The fact is that for so punctilious a presence
Time has some pretty irregular habits
Like someone who has a lot of old
Dry cleaning slips in the bottom of her purse.
Where is that beige wool coat?
Time doesn't return any calls, then pulls
The phone from the wall jack, hurls it through

A closed window and stomps out of the apartment swearing,
"It's forever, you flesh-and-blood fucker, it's forever."
Grief wants some air freshener.
The coffin glows like an old-moneyed smile.

You sit down on a folding chair in the last row
At the poetry reading. A man is decanting
His ironic ambitions. A woman is throwing exquisite
Knives at her hapless childhood. It's not so much
Enlightening as recklessly appalling.
You can respect that.
The art of diceyness lays some rigorous odds.
Afterward the patter starts up again
Like an election campaign or machine
But how else could it be?

You lie awake and polish some words.
You never know when you might want one of them.
In your blue eyes there are no reprobates.
All moments are pickled in this
Ingenuous, articulate brine.
It's neither reassuring nor unkind.
Everything will be open again in the morning.
You might sleep sometime.

January

"Cold as the moon," he'd mutter
In the January of 5 A.M. and 15 below
As he tried to tease the old Chev into greeting
One more misanthropic morning.

It was an art (though he never
Used that curious word) as he thumped
The gas pedal and turned the key
So carefully while he held his breath
And waited for the sharp jounce
And roar of an engaged engine.

"Shoulda brought in the battery last night."
"Shoulda got up around midnight
And turned it over once."

It was always early rising as he'd worked
A lifetime "in every damn sort
Of damn factory." Machines were
As natural to him as dogs and flowers.
A machine as he put it, "was sensible."

I was so stupid about valves and intakes
He thought I was some religious type.
How had I lived as long as I had
And remained so out of it?
And why had I moved of my own free will

To a place that prided itself
On the blunt misery of January?

"No way to live," he'd grumble
As he poked a finger into the frozen throat
Of an unwilling carburetor.
His breath hung in the air
Like a white balloon.

Later on the way to the town
Where we worked while the heater
Wheezed fitfully and the windshield
Showed indifference to the defroster,
He'd turn to me and allow that
The two best things in this world
Were hot coffee and winter sunrises.
The icy road beckoned to no one,
Snow began to drift down sleepily,
The peace of servitude sighed and dreamed.

Les Demoiselles

I walk in the bank to deposit
A pension check first thing
In the morning and the tellers are all

Fresh and made-up with that care
I have always marveled at and they are
Standing there waiting and

I choose Cindy who smiles
Completely, a flower-in-midsummer smile,
Full of light and youth and as much

Joy as could be in a brick building
And I think back to a brothel
I used to go to in France right after

The war. It's not a wicked thought
And not because I'm old and it's
A memory but because I remember

The sight of those women in a more-
Or-less row and their looking at me
With amiable contempt, feigned longing

And unfeigned worldliness. I was a man,
They were women, that was the end of it.
I say "Good morning" to her smile

And I can feel her voice take on a calm
Pleasure as if she's looking into what once
Was there and wondering and looking

Again at the shuffling old-guy presenting
His check and hearing in his voice
The echo of a long-standing sentiment.

Fatality

I was in the store buying the usual—
Coffee, gas, the paper—when I heard
Sonny Parlin's voice on the scanner that
Dave Massenger had barricaded himself
In his house and there were staties everywhere.

Some nightmares you dream in advance and then
Walk into them as they play themselves out
To the final card in the inexorable deck.
Dave started shooting; a marksman (who was
Also a 'Nam vet) drilled him. One shot in the head.

It was front page the next day and the day after
It was a tractor-trailer tipping over on
The Interstate and the day after that a guy
Shot his ex-wife in the parking lot outside
Kmart and after that I lost track.

It was weeks before I went over to see
His wife, Maria. She was sitting in the kitchen
Drinking a cup of herbal tea. The leaves
Were gone off the trees and the sky was that
Autumnal electric blue and the wind was blowing

Hard and fresh out of Canada. "He saw a lot
Of wicked shit," she said. "He'd visited hell
But he'd put it behind him. I mean he was living

With life, putting one foot before the other,
Not trying too hard to be too good."

My eyes strayed around the room and wound up
Resting on a high school photo that had to
Have been Dave, one of those goggle-eyed
Pictures from the senior yearbook. He was
In-country not more than a year later.

Maria started talking about their trip
To Disney World and how Dave had gone
Up to Mickey Mouse and given him a big
Fat kiss. We laughed, then felt the silence.
It was going to start snowing soon.

Draft Morning (1969)

I'd been taking low dosage downers for a few years—
Not to the point of being melodramatically
Addicted but not able to look life in the face
Without the helpful hand of pharmacology either.
And I'd been talking to a shrink who kept
An unlit cigar in his mouth and went to Wellfleet
For a month in the summer and who nodded
Occasionally as I babbled and even less
Occasionally asked me a question—"When did
That happen, Baron" or "Who said that to you?"—
That upon later reflection seemed so mundane
As to make my stomach churn with grief.

A cushioned hell, my mother dying of cancer in bits
And pieces, beached on a hospital bed, her eyes
Empty, her spirit buried beneath painkillers
So that she seemed an ethereal zombie or a super-
Annuated piece of machinery, a relic of a purpose.
And the war that followed you into the grocery store
Checkout aisle so that when I looked up from the jars
Of gefilte fish for my grandmother and the newest
Sugar-dosed cereals for my younger sisters,
There were the newsmagazines with photos of leaders,
Helicopters and increasingly, snapshots from
High school yearbooks of guys who'd been blown away.
We knew, of course, what we were doing. That's what
The living have the right to say although I wasn't much
Of a true believer and one day when I picked up

My Dodge Dart at the garage where I'd had the brake
Shoes replaced, Joe Flaherty, the family mechanic whom
I'd known since childhood asked me how I was doing
And in response, out of the exasperated blue, I said,
"The war bites it" and he walked around the counter,
Put his face directly up to mine and told me
I was a poor excuse for an American,
That brave men were dying in that jungle this minute
While I spouted my two-bit opinions. I thought
There was more sadness in his voice than rage.

One cool, celestially clear autumn morning
When I walked into a downtown building that seemed
Like a cross between an old hotel and an armory,
I wasn't afraid or confident but numb and zoned out.
There was instant camaraderie and instant wariness
And most of all a lot of scoffing among the guys
In the endless lines because that's really all
A nineteen-year-old can do is scoff at the solemn weight
On his tender shoulders, scoffing at death and the army
And girlfriends and parents and other guys, scoffing
At everything. When I looked in the eyes of the bored
And harassed army shrink, I knew I was at one
Of those bridges that takes you somewhere you didn't know
About or even want to know about if you were willing
To step out of line and be half-honest with yourself.
I told him I couldn't do it, and he said in a voice
Just like his eyes, "Is that so, son? Is that so?"
And jotted something on a carbon paper form,
Then blurted "next" as he motioned me away
From his uncluttered desk.

                    Three blocks north in the pale,
Late-afternoon light I threw a vial of pills
Into the gutter—a self-conscious, self-loathing gesture.
I sat a long time at the steering wheel,
Not turning the key, quivering like some bug
In its inordinate flight.

Acting Out

If inappropriateness was the unwanted genius
   Of the scarifying Sixties, the sacrifice of modest,
Melting pot cohesion for the passion of
   The unmoored moment, then my acned, "its-a-sign
Of-virility" friend John Hanscomb was an arbiter,
   Avatar and aviator of experiences so purposefully
Edgy that falling off third-story balconies
   Seemed a relief compared to the confrontations
That were for John the routinely hair-raising
   Hoodoo that made the drabness of our similar
Physical and mental equipment somewhat tolerable
   As when he entered a honky-tonk in south
Baltimore and proceeded to rail in an increasingly
   Southern-Comfort-soaked voice about the ungodly puling
Whininess of country western music. At first
   People showed very faint smiles but as John
Pushed his rant further (harpooning icons like
   Patsy Cline) I could feel the ugliness condense
Like snow clouds. It was only the ministering
   Angel of a bartender who said, "The door's over
There, kid," then pulled out some humongous
   Smith-and-Wesson-type revolver which he aimed
At John's person that saved us from another
   Emergency room sit-in.
                     Or when John would put
On his astronaut suit (right down to the bubble helmet)
   And go to the bank to cash a check and make
Small talk about how degraded life on earth was becoming,

How we Americans were awfully lucky to be
Exploring space because this planet was going
   To be history "pretty darn soon" as he tried to
Expressively snap his heavily gloved fingers.
   His accent was Midwestern techno-geek,
Down-home with an interstellar echo.

   Not far along the path into the disco woods of
The Seventies John met heroin and lost among
   Other traits his socially unsocial sense of humor.
You couldn't even say he died young since he was
   A "half-assed ancient" as he once put it.
We'd get stoned and read *The Narrow Road to the Deep North*
   And talk about how Basho was on such friendly
Terms with fleas and mud. We pictured ourselves
   Tramping America's byways and writing haiku
That we posted on town bulletin boards beside papers
   About fishing licenses and AA meetings.

That the road doesn't go
   On forever, that it barely makes it over the next hill,
Doesn't take away from how John lived for those moments
   When people's eyes started to yeast with startled
Incomprehension and they looked hard at him as if
   To make sure he was there in front of them and not
Somehow elsewhere. I think he loved them then—
   Not their confusion but their coiled souls, their spark.

196

Route One-Thirty

Empty as the apartment to which she drives home
And frank as death, the winter evening falls
Calmly over Route One-Thirty.
The car spins measurably and the few
French fries remaining from her drive-thru lunch
Smell nasty. Were they food?
Would ants treasure them? She winces at
The outside air that stabs her through a bit
Of window she has left healthily open.
The air almost arctic tonight yet

The road so cheerful, so superbly lit,
The river of cars flowing peacefully
As if in thematic concert.
Above the neon signs darkness begins
And that is comforting too somehow,
The finality of it, the limited range
Of emphatic claims—
Eat Here, Buy This, See That.
Look a few feet higher and the written
Voices have vanished. She's between

Marriages or above the exclamations of love
Or bemused to the point of crying (later) into
Her microwaved soup. Now she is driving
And the air is cold and the sky black
And she sings to herself a song
From childhood about a spellbound princess,

For she is tired from her work
And accountably sad and surprised
That even tonight in her six-cylinder skull
Nothing wants banishing or getting right.

Portrait of the Artist

I woke in the bitter, dark, winter morning.
I was eight.

There were the smells of the cat who slept
In my room on a braided rug, of eggs being fried

In the kitchen down the hall, of flannel pajamas,
Of the apartment's mahogany air.

There was dressing and then there was school.
I had hands but lacked the capable motions.

I staggered and stuttered, unkempt as a mongrel.
I dreaded putting on the one light in my little room,

A table lamp shaped like an old New York City skyscraper.
Light was so nasty.

There was the blue smell of cold pipes.
I had to get up.

Why didn't familiarity make anything easier?
Putting my socks on, combing my hair, deciding

Which of three pairs of identical shoes I should wear...
I held my hands before me

Like some sort of faith healer.
I looked at the mezzotint on the wall of Christ.

He was so sweet and baleful.
He was so little help to me.

Winter was a cap your mother had knit that you
Didn't want to wear because it was unmanly.

Winter was a grudge.
Winter was the silent type like Brother James

Who never spoke when he thrashed you.
I went to the window and breathed upon it

And traced my initials in the beautiful steam.
My father called. My day was done.

The Great Depression

The glow of pennies in a quart canning jar
The glow of the numinous wooden radio
The glow of late May...
It was as though a giant had swallowed an era whole

And all the people and trees and buildings
And dogs and cats
Lived there in his stomach.
It was as if time were a parent

Placing a permanent hand on your shoulder....
Definition is a horizon
Even dreams must obey
As they exalt on another plane the burnished day.

Banks moaned, armies rattled,
The fireflies danced and the snow fell
As children lay patiently in their beds
Waiting for a tale that sweetly murdered time....

Once there was a little man with a mustache
Who could roar like an aeroplane.
He lived in a topsy-turvy house on a dismal street
Beside a canal full of oak leaves....

In the middle of the confining night
A nexus of human nerves awakens,

Worried and fretful yet warm,
Cozy as a coin in a rich man's pocket.

Outside on the street or prairie
There is no outside....
The giant relaxes and sings a polka-like song
About a little man with a mustache

Who stamps his feet on the speaker's platform
Like an angry pony....
There are cheers like fields of wheat.
Then everyone sleeps.

For the Yiddish Poets

Poof poof poof! Languages people cities
Gone in the breadth of a cat's whisker,
Gone in a tyrant's belch,
Gone in a terse goodnight.
I blinked one morning while rising from bed
And a phrase I had honed for three insomniac hours
Vanished. Where is the tissue paper of eternity
That might wrap our hapless largesse?

Poof poof poof!
I sneezed on the El and my droplets dispersed
Among the throng of grunting, shaky humanity.
In two weeks a fever fells a butcher in the Bronx.
"Never sick a day in his murderous life,"
His wife swears over coffee to a neighbor
Who shakes her head and mumbles a prayer.

Poof poof poof!
Typhoid Annie was a Jew, one of the prophets
Awaiting entry into the latter-day Torah,
One of the festering saints who polished
Misfortune till it glowed like a malignant ruby.

Poof poof poof!
My huzzahs have a Fourth-of-July, *goyishe*,
Patriotic, *shikse*-loving ring to them.
My tongue hungers for blueberry pie, ballpark hot dogs,
The tangy, cloying fizz of a slightly warm cola.

My tongue greets English with the vociferous
Friendliness of a vote-cadging alderman. I favor
Mongrel languages spoken by demonstrative recalcitrants.

Poof poof poof!
I spill a *bissel* coffee on the counter of a restaurant
On Second Avenue and within seconds a waitress
Smiles at my clumsiness and wipes the surface clean
With a damp cloth she can twirl like a lariat.
What might emerge from those drops? They disappear no more
Than the souls of our forebears disappeared, than our tears
In Egypt disappeared, than our hovel in the Pale of Settlement
That was torched in a pogrom disappeared. Are you acquainted
With ashes? They rise in the air but then settle
On the earth: they are underfoot this very moment.
They are speaking to one another. Whether you know
Their language or not is immaterial. They know yours.

Poof poof poof!
Sorrow dissolves in the chicken fat of daylight, the horns
Of taxicabs, a fat, old *patzer* standing at a street corner puffing
On a stogie, a poet clairvoyant with passion thrusting a piece
Of paper into a friend's hand. Read this read this read this!

A Roman

Lately Gaius Claudius
Has grown weary of his dreams.
It isn't the tedium of adulteries
Or the malice of murder that troubles him;
It's the pettiness and multitude of his desires,
How they insert themselves into every nook
Of his nocturnal mind, forcing him in ardent,
Unflinching detail to betray secrets, steal coins,
Fib for no reason, drink beyond satiation.

A victim of his itinerant sensations, he sees
The Christians differently, their pallor
And their fierceness—worthless wisdom he hates.
A body of iron with handsome wounds
From many campaigns and a mind
Soft as sheep's guts. How?

He rises in the morning haggard and unfit.
He strolls through the city that
Made him a man, saluting his equals,
Knowing that they observe the marks of his distress.
When he finds himself by the river,
He wonders about those ghostly longings the Christians
Love to incite, of their all-seeing god and their trust
In the strength of unsanctioned rites.

The sun glances playfully off the sedate water.
He lowers his head as if in obeisance,
As if to heal what he cannot protect.

Immolation (Saigon, 1964)

...and what I, as a raw scoffing
Know-it-all adolescent, saw in the photos
Was horror that had nothing to do
With movie screens but something for which
I mercifully had no words although
The feeling of that deliberateness,
Of going about the preparations to set oneself
On fire and the imagined actual moment of the match
Engulfed me for endless seconds in a dizzying
Dread so that when the toaster clunked
Or the coffeepot began to burble I looked up
And regarded them as if they were artifacts
Of the afterlife and felt my sight no longer was
Human vision but the insight of unearthliness.
I then went on about my day and forgot,
As we are prone to say when we remember,
But what forgetting was there for anyone
Who looked however closely at that sight?

Decades later, I see at random moments
That photo-moment and glimpse in the space
That time has made a peace
Without zones, pacts or delegates,
That springs from not dissembling
Or flinching or louring or even lamenting but
Stepping into the fire that is there always—
The consuming roar of finitude—
And embracing it completely

As the odor of gasoline floods the nostrils
And the scratching match is calm thunder.
In that absolute moment of the lighting
Are all moments and I vow again
To shut my shifting mouth before the fire
And the life—so many moments—that disappears
Like wars or photos or the darkest
Most acrid flames.
                    The candor
Of suffering survives....

From *Subject Matter* (2004)

Global Warming

Mumbling and joking, we hearken to pains
That fester in the comfort of unseasonable weather.
Our time is short—precisely. Uncertainties
Condole misgivings while we idle

In infinite traffic, drumming on plastic
And imbibing sundry pert yet patient voices:
"Your forecast"... and the sun made for a beach day.
How is that the blanket protecting us

Feels more electric every year? Too many errands,
Too many longings—we could recount
Our downpours for hours but no one is asking.
We outlive insects but not trees.
Rocks are eternity. No snow tonight.
We unbutton a button, feel clammy and comment.

Anti-Depressant

What a pig happiness is. Plus,
I'm a body living with an anti-body.
You probably don't know how that goes—
Bound and unbound at the same ill time.

The pills hold sincerity down.…
Once, I bled a true blue-streak; now
I reference mute science shyly as
The next penitent. I'm chemical

And it hurts. The calibrations shine then dull;
R&D works overtime. I should be pleased
And some days am. It wavers and feints
And my smile is ghastly but I can walk down
A street and see the ratty English sparrows
Forage in the litter and not start to cry.

Buddhism

It's about not-about. I'll start again
And stop there—which is more like it.
The Via Negativa goes Nowhere
And that's a lovely place—the empty lake

In front of the barren hotel where some timeless,
Karmic habitués look past one another.
Better five minutes of Zen than
A hundred books about Zen. Poems

Are another story. They too inhabit
No place gracefully, dwell
Offhandedly in mini-eternities.
They too welcome oblivion. Authorship's
A ruse but that fades. Sit still again.
No nothing. You can feel it. Approximately.

Trucking

"He's right good-humored when he's not surly,"
That's Peckerwood describing J.D., though
It could be Moonwalk divining Bear Man,
Or Dropkick on Tail Feather. Thousands of miles

Space a mind out until there are gaps that feel
Like whole time zones; you forget who's waiting
Back home or that there is a back home.
When you're sitting in East Zip getting weighed

Or a waitress forgets it was a double cheeseburger,
Your head springs back like a rubber band
And you feel how damn tired the body is
That supports your drifting mind. And when you call
Home and she's supposed to be there and she isn't,
Every crappy, twanging song becomes your own.

Romance

Cutting through the fogbanks of urbanity
Takes more than one but less than two martinis.
Within that zone the glimmer of a smile
Begins that might come to illumine a heart—

A metonymy for the random rivers
Of feeling coursing through human bodies.
Dim lights, extended hands above then
Below the table, a murmuring piano:

No wonder the moment is fêted while
The lifetime is consigned to duration's
Gray dustbin. Outside, traffic throbs,
Newsboys rumor, dusk settles into
Vacant evening. Simultaneously, both
People say something tender but witty.

Karma (II)

Driving home from the second shift and thinking
About how Sandy Banks is always
Late on her paperwork, she sees a car
Heading toward her, going the wrong way

Up the ramp fast. She jerks onto the shoulder.
In a dark wind the car shoots by. No one's
Behind her and when she turns her neck around
To see, the car is gone already. She feels

A chill take hold of her; then she's shaking
And crying. The engine keeps muttering, muttering.
So strange, how her last thoughts
And final moments were like the rest
Of life, rooted in a deep narrowness.
She exhales, squints—no lights before her.

Blurbs

"Stylish" means not hopelessly hokey.
"Radiant" means uplift.
"Brilliant" means hyper-articulate
But vastly uncommunicative.

"Brave" means still breathing.
"Big-hearted" means fuzzy.
"Dynamic" means overbearing.
"Wise" means self-satisfied.

"Taking risks" means receives a check
Biweekly but pays homage to
Rimbaud in a veiled corner of the soul.
"Triumphant" means a hack who hung in there.
"Luminous" see "Radiant."
"Bravo!" means I'm done with words.

Great Plains

As children we lay on the ground and let the wind
Flow over us. On our backs we gazed up at
The deep-seated sky and felt dust darken our eyes.
On our stomachs we gripped the earth and heard

The ground groan. When we returned to our homes
That huddled beside a few spindly trees,
We felt abandoned: any edifice seemed false.
The Technicolor sunsets ridiculed us.

How to stand up? How to take the wind in your chest
And not huff and choke? When Henry Spotted Horse
Collapsed on Main Street one autumn afternoon,
I looked down cautiously. His eyes were staring
In different directions. "Son, you have to live for
Hundreds of years before you know anything."

Farmhouses, Iowa

Invariably, a family in each one
And someone opening the fridge to fetch
A carton of milk, someone sitting in
A chair and shelling peas, someone looking

Out a window at a barn, two willow trees.
Solitude broods like a pursuing shadow;
A radio fades in and out—the voice
Eager yet eerie. Three ages anchor

The oaken dinner table: Mom and Dad
Up-before-dawn weary, Grandma perturbed
About half-thawed rolls, the children recounting
School stories, then silent. In the parlor
A whiskey tumbler rests beside a Bible.
The old collie whimpers when a car goes by.

Journey to the East

The guru was too fond of antitheses—
The further this / the less that—
For my hardened taste, but when we sat
Stilly I felt an unconcern for the clamor

Inside me that answers whatever
Cognition the world proposes.
An ant walked along his arm and he
Asked of it, "Who are you?" Stock wisdom

But he didn't move to brush the creature away.
Say, you or I are that ant crawling
Across a soft, somewhat hairy surface
And our instincts lie in our being alive
And that is all we know. What name is there?
What if great love is anonymous?

Tragedy

Imagine the land, rock, sky placing a hand
On you that won't let go, that confines you
Amid awful vastness. The boasts proclaiming
Destiny whimper. The coyotes call

No one's Christian name; any answer
Is dumb as tumbleweed and cold as nightfall.
When a hero appears, the gathered
Soldiers are more sullen than vengeful.

The dignity of the dispossessed dogs them;
The jokes about braves and squaws
Never placate them. Even death fails.
When Crazy Horse stands before the flag-topped fort,
They wonder what led them to this time-scoured spot
And whether his fierce eye will ever leave them.

Blues

Blues came round and knocked on my back door
Oh blues came round and knocked on my back door
Hello, Mister Blues, I've seen you before

Some folks' kindness always comes with a speech
Oh some folks' kindness always comes with a speech
Every long day, they got something to preach

My woman left me, that's a natural fact
Oh my woman left me, that's a natural fact
She told me her good heart is not coming back

Talking and drinking only make it worse
Oh talking and drinking only make it worse
You enter naked and you leave in a hearse

Morning and evening are a dance on hard ground
Oh morning and evening are a dance on hard ground
A power you borrow before you go down

Commune

"Energy Parcel Passing Through" was how
Arnie Elfman, also known as Cosmo,
Designated himself—as in "I'm just
An Energy Parcel Passing Through but I think...."

We bore with it, since all of us were indulging
Some species of spiritual quixotism
But one evening after a typical day
Of fixing broken machines, random squabbling,

Whole grains and weather watching, Kate Scharf
Told Arnie/Cosmo/Energy she was tired
Of his self-conscious unconsciousness: "Who
In the name of Vishnu do you think you are?"
Arnie smiled cryptically and left the next morning.
He'd never been much help milking the goats.

Opinion

Halfway to work and Merriman already has told me
What he thinks about the balanced budget, the Mets'
Lack of starting pitching, the dangers of displaced
Soviet nuclear engineers, soy products and diesel cars.

I look out the window and hope I'll see a swan.
I hear they're bad-tempered but I love their necks
And how they glide along so sovereignly.
I never take the time to drive to a pond

And spend an hour observing swans. What
Would happen if I heeded the admonitions of beauty?
When I look over at Merriman, he's telling Driscoll
That the President doesn't know what he's doing
With China. "China," I say out loud but softly.
I go back to the window. It's started snowing.

Melancholy

Weakness—the pale succumbing to loneliness,
Refusing to admit anyone else, indulging
The blue perquisites of adolescence
Long past their sensible deliquescence.

He knew it but went on drinking and regretting,
Not calling his friends and regretting,
Making scenes over nothing and regretting.
It helped to make him despise himself,

Which was, he sensed, what he wanted. He was
Then, in his oblique way, at ease to wander
The city's brazen or quiet streets, conjuring
Random lives and how the slim arc
Of emotion was pulverized. Back home, he put
On some Monk, lay down, half-cried.

Haberdasher

Over the course of decades style changed:
Your regular Joe stopped wearing hats,
Polished brogues, ties, starched white shirts.
America became casual and drove away

From the store on the corner of First and Main.
Even Sunday faded. Over his after-hours Scotch
The retailer pleaded to his pleated wife:
"What can I do when gentlemen no longer

Are gentlemen? What can I say to a world of rubes?"
Each morning he tied a perfect Windsor knot.
Later, he stared disconsolately out the windows
At the busy cars, brightened when a face appeared.
"How could you buy a suit from a stranger?"
He asked himself. Each advertised day replied.

Radio

One educated voice—no drawl or chipped vowels
Or hurried elisions or wobbly ethnic inflections—
Is taking with another educated voice
About the Saudis. I think No Jews Allowed,

Camels, petro plutocrats, holy cities,
Kings, covered-up women. "Short-term strategy,"
One voice is intoning. I love how they calmly
Ratiocinate. Now and then, a bubble of wit

Trembles wisely. I could listen to their savvy
For hours—the semi-thinking person's narcotic.
When, for the hell of it, I push a random button,
The Mamas and the Papas are sublimely harmonizing.
They sound like angels on drugs. I sing too. Why talk,
When you can rise on longing's crazy wings?

From *Carthage* (2005)

Carthage and Airplanes

Carthage likes to ride in airplanes.
Up in the sky he can forget
About the schedules of earth.
It is almost like thinking,
Gazing out the window at the clouds.

He likes to ponder.
"We're pretty high up," he says
To his aides.
"I wonder if we could go much higher."
Everyone looks thoughtful.

Back on earth ten-year-olds heft Uzis,
People drop dead on sidewalks,
Friendship sours like old milk.
How much better it is in the sky!

Too bad you have to be going somewhere.
Too bad the endless limo will appear
And some suit or turban or daishiki
Will greet you and start
Telling you about what's going
To happen soon or happened yesterday.

"Why don't you fly around more?"
Carthage would like to say to them.

If you live in the sky, nothing happens.
You don't even see the rain.
It is almost like thinking.

Carthage and the Evil

Carthage is sorting out the bad
        From the evil,
A task that could give God a headache.
Carthage shoulders on,
        Searching for criteria:
When the evil obliterate a village
They brag about it,
        Whereas the bad snivel
And protest that the blood on their hands
Is dye, that they too are victims,
        That the ax of reason is an equivocal tool.

Distinctions are dubious
        But some rule of thumb is required.
Without distinctions you'd be at it forever.

Carthage finds solace imagining
        The demise of the evil.
They will be standing in a room screaming
        Or pointing a pistol at the sky.
The ceiling will dance on them.
        Imploded stars will impale them.

        The righteous slaughter the evil
So the bad can live in murderous peace.
        The good, those like the widow's
Three sons who were in the marketplace

Purchasing lentils and chickpeas when the fires descended,
Do not appear in any strategic equations.

The good have no ambassadors.
They are tasteless as water.
They drudge in the apolitic mills of love.

Look at the evil,
Carthage is saying to the bad.
I am measuring their tyranny.
It is like a shoe size.
You better talk to your miserable human feet
That always are growing.

Carthage's Diary

Time is looking over his shoulder
And talking trash about tomorrow.
Like steam, Carthage feels he is evaporating.

He keeps a diary to hold his importance in place.
He is building a little monument.
The problem is he doesn't know what to say.

He could write about what he had for breakfast.
He had an extra waffle with that good artificial syrup on it.
He has to confess that seems trivial.

Everyone eats waffles.
He's given orders to invade a few countries.
That's not something everyone has done.

It doesn't feel like much, though.
You're excited for a few days
And then you're back to thinking about waffles.

He can't walk in and start talking waffles
To the generals and admirals.
They want to talk about battlefields.

Death is taking super-sized bites out of time.
Tall monuments have been blown up.
Carthage sighs. He can erase everything.

Carthage Plays Cards

Every other week Carthage has some buddies—
   Al, Joe, Brownie and Jim—
      Over for a game of poker.
Don't stay up he tells the First Lady—
   Not that they would have sex anyway.

  For years she has kept
    Her desires to herself.
Maybe they drowned
And will wash up on the shores of history
    Decades from now. Long after her death,
Small defiant cries will be heard
      Echoing in a dark archive.

Now there are potato chips, beer
      And playing cards with naughty ladies
  On their backs.
  "Wouldn't I like to have a piece of that," Al says.
The guys have jokes to tell.
Brownie is laughing so hard Budweiser
  Is shooting out his nose.

Carthage's wife wakes to their chortling din.
    She thinks about appearing in her nightgown,
Leaving a few buttons open, eyeing them calmly.
    She knows they would sober up instantly.
"Evening, ma'am," they would bleat like Boy Scouts.

She pulls the covers over her head.
She tries to burrow into a small dream—
A small house in a small town
Where she could live quietly.

Carthage puts his cards face up.
     "Straight flush!" he hollers.
The others holler too.
     Nothing feels this good.

Carthage's Advisors

Each day Carthage sees his advisors.
They know more than he does but are polite about it.
They smile handsomely; their voices are intelligent honey.
Carthage gets sick of it.
He can make audiences of patriots
And rich Christians go crazy but he gets tired of listening
Like some kind of educated monkey.

He wishes one of them would shoot from the hip,
"Look, Carthage, you don't know shit about this
And if you don't care to know anything
Just sign on the line and save us the time."
As it is, he has to consider options,
Nod his head like a weary bear,
Periodically thrust his body forward
And plant his elbows on his desk to show
He is engaged and forceful.

His young male advisors have nicknames like "Chip."
Even the black one from Georgia Tech
Answers to something like that—"Rip," or maybe, "Kip."
The women, he's noticed, tend to be a little flat chested,
Probably from being so brainy.
Here they all are—talking to someone
Who barely passed "Intro to Western Civ."
He liked the course actually but he had a heavy girlfriend
That semester. Dawn Something-or-Other.
When they fucked, she flung her arms all over the place.

A couple of times she bopped him on the chin.
He kind of liked it.

Occasionally, to keep them honest,
He brings up what seems to him an apposite figure—
"Is this guy some kind of Hitler?"
"I don't think Patton would have backed down."
"Lincoln used to think long and hard before he spoke."
His advisors look at him with a blend of interest and misgiving
As if he were a horse that had bolted from a paddock.

His point about whatever personage he's cited dwindles.
Everyone waits.
Carthage furrows his brow like a third-rate actor
To show that he can deliberate.
"Is that clear?" he inquires.
Everyone scurries and chirps brightly
As if history were alive.

Carthage Gets Mail

Citizens write letters to Carthage.
Mostly they want a smiling signed photograph.
A husband or wife may leave,
The IRS may be auditing them,
The car may be broke,
But the President is there smiling.

Now and then Carthage likes to stroll
Among the eager interns filling envelopes.
He's not a Catholic but he feels like the Pope,
The way they want him to put a hand on their shoulders
And say a word to them.

He stops at one desk where a young woman
Is reading a letter someone has written by hand.
It's blue ballpoint and looks hasty.
It's not really a letter, just one line—
 "What do you do with the dead children?"
Someone has written asking him that—
"What do you do with the dead children?"

Carthage shakes his head—
There are going to be people who don't understand what war is,
People who are weak and confused,
People who think the world should be perfect.

The young woman looks up tentatively at Carthage.
"Here," he says, "let me personally sign

That photograph." She nods thankfully.
Carthage writes his name over the signature
That already is embossed on his picture.
He has to admit he looks pretty snazzy in that picture.

The interns are all watching him.
The young woman's lips are pursed as if she is going
To start crying from gratitude.
Carthage smiles easily
And waves a hand for the camera that never grieves.

Carthage among School Children

He doesn't have to listen to pleas concerning
Tax breaks, public works, judgeships, laws,
Missiles, policies, more and more money....
No manically firm handshakes squeeze him.
The smiles and voices aren't turned up to ten:

You are the greatest man and I am
The greatest man and if there were a woman
In the room, she would be the greatest woman.
Carthage gets tired of being superlative.
He remembers when his father took him aside

And told him he was an asshole from whom
He expected nothing. "Do you understand, boy?
I'll spell it—A-S-S-H-O-L-E."
Carthage understood. He remembers staring at
His father's well-polished loafers.

Now, Carthage reads a book to a classroom of children
About a mole and a rabbit.
They are friends despite their different personalities—
Mole is plodding and secretive,
Rabbit is always blurting out his feelings.

Carthage wonders whether he is the mole or the rabbit.
Maybe he's both.
He looks from the book to the children.

242

Like saints in frescos, calm light glows in
Their rapt faces.

Perhaps he should keep a couple of children
Around his office.
"Here," he would say to other leaders,
"Are some of my friends.
We all like the book about the mole and the rabbit."

"Grow up" is time's favorite expletive.
Carthage tells the class to come visit him
Whenever they are in the capital.
When the children applaud, their eager hands
Are hope's confetti.

Carthage Hears about His Name

It shouldn't have happened but it did.
One day on the radio Carthage heard
A British voice that an American barely
Could understand talking about
A place called "Carthage."
It was destroyed.
Not once but twice:
First by Romans and then by Arabs.
Carthage looked out the car window
As if the trees and houses might console him.
Quickly he flipped the dial.
The Turtles were singing "Happy Together."

That was better
But Carthage wondered
Why he was named for a destroyed city.
How could he be descended from something
That had been destroyed?
Why had Carthage made so much trouble for itself?
He had to pull the car off the Interstate
And take some deep breaths.

A voice told him he should turn
The radio on and find out what happened next.
Another voice
Told him probably there was a city
There now with shopping malls and parking lots.
That was how things worked.

Everything came back.
It didn't matter what you did
Because everything came back.

Carthage turned the ignition key and began
Drumming with his index fingers on the dashboard.
"So happy together," he sang.
He felt mystical and free
Or maybe forgetful.

Before they were destroyed
What songs had the people of Carthage sung?
They must have been happy.
They must have.

Maisie Wormser

The Author

Baron Wormser is the author of seven books of poetry, a poetry chapbook, a collection of short stories, a memoir, and is the coauthor of two books about teaching poetry. He directs the Frost Place Conference on Poetry and Teaching and teaches in the Stonecoast MFA Program. He is the recipient of fellowships from the National Endowment for the Arts and the John Simon Guggenheim Memorial Foundation and served as Poet Laureate of Maine from 2000 to 2005. He lives with his wife in Cabot, Vermont.